PATH OF
DIRTY SOLES

PATH OF DIRTY SOLES

· ·

Ray Robles

XULON PRESS

Xulon Press
2301 Lucien Way #415
Maitland, FL 32751
407.339.4217
www.xulonpress.com

Unless otherwise indicated, Scripture quotations taken from the English Standard Version (ESV). Copyright © 2001 by Crossway, a publishing ministry of Good News Publishers. Used by permission. All rights reserved.

Paperback ISBN-13: 978-1-6628-3021-1
Ebook ISBN-13: 978-1-6628-3022-8

In Dedication to Frances Hernandez:

Thank you for your prayers, your patience, and continual support. You are God's maid servant.

Table of Contents

THE JOURNEY

. . . .

"The path of the Christian is not always bright with sunshine; he has his seasons of darkness and of storm. True, it is written in God's Word, "His ways are ways of pleasantness, and all His paths are peace... the dearest of his children must bear the cross."

Charles Spurgeon, Morning and Evening[1]

A journey is described by many delineating characteristics: an adventure, a caravan, an excursion, an exploration, a pilgrimage, a sojourn, a voyage.[2] If we stopped for a moment to consider their common denominator, we would find

---

[1]   Spurgeon, Charles, (April 29). *Morning and Evening*. 2nd ed. Massachusetts: Hendrickson Publishers, 1991.

[2]   "Journey." <u>The American Heritage Dictionary fo the English Language</u>. 4th ed. 2000, p. 749.

these descriptions are all synonymous to another term to describe a journey; motion. However, all of these characteristics do not definitively explain what a journey is. Moreover, if a journey is defined by its motion, then those of us who find ourselves at a halt would be considered journey-less.

Furthermore, none of these depictions indicate destination. A journey could not be complete without a destination. Just because we are moving in a direction does not mean we are heading in a destination. Just as, being still does not not mean we are not moving towards a direction.

There is another depiction used to describe a journey, it is called "wandering."[3] Wandering is similar to a journey in that it projects motion. Yet, wandering is unsettled movement, a drifting, or a deviating from one direction to another. Ironically, wandering is devoid of a destination. So, if wandering is lacking destination, wouldn't wandering be the very opposite of a journey? Thus, to think of wandering as a proper characteristic used to describe a journey is to embrace the idea that life is a random series of events that will eventually be the very causes to bring about a purposeful destination. And if this is so, one must conclude

---

[3]   Ibid., "wandering," p. 1544.

that even in wandering there is a destination one must choose.

Life is a wandering until we are awakened by the unveiled truth found in Jesus Christ. It is at the cross where we stop wandering, and are set on a course towards a destination. The cross, however, is not the beginning of the journey. Although we are set on a path towards eternity, our journey does not actually begin at salvation. We are just removed from the wandering and set towards a direction.

Now, please allow me to make one thing completely clear. Accepting Jesus Christ never comes with a catch but there is a contingency. Jesus does desire to be our savior. But He longs to be our Lord, as well. Here is where the rubber meets the road.

It is easy to be a Christian under Jesus our savior. Why? The experienced favor of unmerited Grace, the satisfying transfusion of Christ's righteousness, and the overwhelming magnitude of His mercy that outweighs all judgement. Regardless of how enormously good and well-serving our intentions prove, we are all deserving of hell. Still, Jesus absolves all of us who come to confession of Christ by erasing the certificate of debt, placing it on the cross, and disarming Satan's power over our lives.[4]

> **To be clear here, WE DID ABSOLUTELY NOTHING to earn this, obtain this, procure this, or retain this. HE DID IT !**
> **And HE DID IT ALL!**

Lord Jesus, however, is of another disposition. Where "Savior" Jesus, *GIVES*, "Lord" Jesus, *TAKES*. Allow me to explain. Savior Jesus gives us newness of life, pardons us from sin, provides us with His Spirit and GIVES us a new nature, and even institutes a little thing called *sanctification* that affords us time to get those faulty areas in our lives corrected. Moreover, Savior Jesus does this without a single demand or a contingency. We gain all these wonderful fringe benefits without a single need to do anything to earn them.

In contrast, Lord Jesus *TAKES*. He takes away our self-desires, self-determinations, self-wants, self-wills and exchanges them with self-awareness, self-meekness, selflessness, and emptiness of self. Lord Jesus is unlike "Savior" Jesus, in that, Lord Jesus has a condition. Lord Jesus demands full surrender of ourselves. Now, here is the thing

---

4   Holy Bible: (Colossians 2.13) Christian Standard Bible. Tennessee: Holman Bible Publishers.

about the type of surrender Lord Jesus demands: it's a surrender that is an all-encompassing discipline of, not only conduct and practice, but also of correction and acceptance of consequence. Anyone of us who desires to become Christ's follower, must deny ourselves, take up our crosses daily, and follow Him.[5] Surrendering to Christ's lordship requires our cross.

> **Salvation was Christ's cross.**
> **Discipleship is our cross.**

The cross of salvation took Christ's life. The cross of discipleship takes ours. We cannot even begin to follow Jesus until we deny ourselves, pick up our cross, and pick it up daily. Again, at salvation we are taken from the wandering and given direction. Thus, our journey begins not at Christ's cross but when our own cross is picked up.

---

[5] Ibid., Luke 9.23

Introduction

THE RED ROAD

· ·

T his was a first day of new firsts for me. New Jersey was a new state, and my new home was a parsonage for a ministry I was newly hired. What's more, it was the first time I was placed in a position to lead an entire staff.

The para-church ministry I was newly hired for was located in a small town with few sidewalks, unlike New York to which I was accustomed. The parsonage I would move into was surrounded by woods. Along the front side of the parsonage stood a road that stretched from one part of the town to the next. Moreover, a river rested along the right side of the road.

Taking in my new surroundings, I remember thinking "This is a long way from living in New York City Project Housing." As I laughed to myself, I began to survey my new surroundings. Taking in my new living environment, I noticed a path just adjacent to the river. This path was made up of a blush russet color that was produced by the clay-based soil that gave it its reddish-hue.

So, as my eyes traced the serpentine roseate walk way, Holy Spirit made me conscious to His presence when His still soft voice spoke. "Ray, that is how I would like for you to travel to and from the office." Looking back at that moment, I realize God was actually testing me to see if I would be willing to be lead in exactly His way.

When I first set foot on the "Red Road," I became immersed in symbolic imagery that began to inspire creativity, shape ideality, and invent cinematic notions similar to a movie narrator who characterizes the discourse of the main character's events. "He who walks along the crimson path," my tale-teller resonated in my head. However, as the days evolved into weeks, the screen play of my mind slowly began to rewrite its story and my mythological script started to read more like a divine comedy.

At this point, the "Red Road" posed little to be desired. The mile-long stretch began to appear longer, each step laborious, and its role without any apparent purpose. Consequently, I found myself rationalizing this invitation from God as nothing more than a projected romanticism about some anagogic footpath leading into a spiritual dimension that would result in a transmogrified and more evolved version of my Christian self.

Temptation now set in. "Maybe I can start driving in? Yea, I can take the car. This will give me more time. I can sleep in a little longer. I could even grab breakfast to bring to the office, and still have time enough to prepare for the start of my day," I pondered. As I reasoned and I rationalized, I began to rationalize my reasons. And the more that I rationalized a reason, the more I reasoned and rationalized myself into giving in. Soon, I became motivated to do as I had proposed to do... and did it.

My first morning off the path was inaugurated with a much-desired extra half-hour of sleep, followed by a slowly paced morning of preparation. This was accompanied by the grabbing of car keys, cruising down the opposite direction of work campus, stopping by a local deli, purchasing a breakfast sandwich, and a quick detour for an ice coffee.

After grabbing my items, I entered my car and shut the door behind me. As I nestled myself into the contour of my seat, an invasion of darkened clouds thundered, and a rushing whirlwind of emotions eclipsed the plush clear blue sky of my thinking. Instantly, I became consumed with creeping feelings of being *alone*.

These feelings where not the common variety of lonely feelings, nor were they the emotional demands for fellowship. Furthermore, these were not the feelings of alienation. Quite contrary, these were the feelings of being hidden, out of sight, and invisible. I was overwhelmed by this idea that God was no longer look at me, or if He had turned away. Processing this thought, I started to recall Genesis 3.9. It was as if I were Adam and I can hear God's voice saying to me, "Where are you?"

Making my way to the office, those words continued to bounce around my mind. We humans are seldom completely truthful with ourselves. We are honest with our selves, at best, but not always completely truthful. So, as objective as I could possibly be, I began to observe that my convictions were not the feelings of being convicted of a crime, nor where they the feelings of condemnation, or feelings of accusation. In contrast, I was feeling compelled to urgently make a correction. That is when I learned that the convictions of Holy Spirit are always, first, the voice of pronounced certainty that seeks to persuade us towards the Lord's assured position on a matter. Second, it is an instruction leading our codes of conduct to align them with the conduct of His holiness.

"It is not sin that disqualifies you, you can stop playing by sin's rules. It's the principle application of sin and it's practices that disqualify you, the Holy Spirit said."

The darkened skies of my mind erupted into spontaneous bursts of lucidity and perspicuity. My thoughts shifted from a fear to a fervor towards reconciliation. Repentance, I learned, is not only experiencing emotional feelings of regret and remorse for our actions. Repentance is the power source fueling the changed nature we inherit when becoming born again. Repentance is not just the one time experience at our confession of Jesus as our Savior. Repentance is the "already and still doing" practice of our Christian disciple.

In short, we are the "REPENTED" and still "REPENTING."

Needless to say, I WALKED to the office through the red road the next morning.

I wish I could tell you that this was the "*God-instance*" I was longing for. It wasn't. My walk along the path appeared to be the same lengthy, quiet, and uneventful walk it had consistently been. One day, I decided to speed walk through the road, verses my usual prayerful strolling through, when

I noticed the laces of one of my shoes had become unfastened. Moreover, the designer sneakers I decided to wear this day were taking on the tint of the red clay path. And in the "name of fashion," immediate action was required.

Angry with myself for dressing inappropriately to the terrain, I begin to initiate evasive maneuvers to salvage the aesthetic nature of my shoes. Then, the voice of Holy Spirit whispered in my ear. "The one who has bathed needs only to wash his feet."[6] Waves of eroding thoughts poured out of my mind and I went from a perception of things to gaining a proper "perspective" of things.

The Holy Spirit then proceeded to show me how my perceptions restricted me to mere human limitations. He desired for me to gain a perspective which hoists beyond intellectual knowledge to a spiritually ascended understanding. Perspective, as the Spirit began to disclose, is about having the right depths and dimensions. The proper depths and dimensions our Christian lives require can only be defined through properly dividing the Scriptures. Holy Spirit then follows up with this, "You are now walking along the path of dirty soles."

Ephesians 6.15 started resonating in my mind. "Fit your feet with the preparation that

---

[6]   Ibid., John 13

comes from the good news of peace..." The words seemed to appear highlighted in neon as I gained a greater *perspective*. For the first time, it became so clear. The Apostle Paul used the word '*prepare*' when describing how we should cover your feet. Preparation is about anticipation, foresight, and being alert. Furthermore, it is our feet that move us along the path of our journey. It is our feet that walk us into the dark paths, the green pastures, and along the shores of the still waters. It is also our feet that move us through the valley of the shadow of death. Thus, our feet need preparation, refreshing, and washing.

Holy Spirit further showed me that our feet are symbolic to life's journey and the paths. The path we take is indicative to our ability, or our lack of ability, to be lead by the Truth found in accordance to our Lord Jesus Christ, His Word, and the echoing voice of His Spirit. Finally, the washing of our feet represents our willingness to move ourselves towards repentance and recovery.

So, it is with this in mind that I had immersed myself into this journey of life with the Spirit of Lord of Grace and Truth as my only guide.

Chapter 1

THE PIT STOPS

. . . .

L ife elicits encounters, experiences, and events that cause us to naturally act out in accordance to behavior based on perceived emotions of happiness or hurt. There are harsh realities that we will face as Christians. There are circumstances that we will walk into which will cause, create, and confirm feelings that need confession and/or correction. Some of these feelings are based on faulty emotions incorrectly interpreted within us. This is not to say that we cannot feel a certain way or that we can be told that we are wrong for feeling a particular way. However, because we are feeling in a certain manner, does not always make how we feel appropriate for our circumstances.

Pricilla Shirer, in her book *Discerning the Voice of God*, similarly describes the perceptions of our emotions like this...

"Our spirits are the core of who we are. Likewise, every human has a deep inner voice called a conscience. This voice guides and directs our choices... The problem with following [our] conscience is that every person's conscience is formed and developed based on [our] personal environment and specific life circumstances. Each person's conscience has been shaped by the tradition and truth or lie to which it has been exposed."[7]

Psalm 4.4 tells us, "Be angry, do not sin; ponder in your own hearts and on your bed, and be silent."[8] As described, God does not fault us for feeling a certain feeling. However, we are advised to think carefully about it and not allow our emotions to cause us to act out inappropriately. In addition, Jesus tells us, "Out of the heart comes evil..."[9] Simply put, perception of our emotions does not always provide the best rationale.

True Christian life is indicative through our ability to bear actions consistent with our

---

[7] Shirer, Pricilla. Discerning the Voice of God. Tennessee: LifeWay, 2006, p. 32.

[8] Holy Bible, Psalm 4.4

[9] Ibid., Mark 7.21

confession. Some of our perceptions are con-structs of the emotions that became actualized through past pains we experienced. These emotions, over time, condition responses that shape instinctive behavior, and on the basis of these perceptions we determine happiness or hurt. The principle governing perception of happiness or hurt is a principle called association.

Gerald G. May, in his book "Addictions and Grace," explains it this way: "new patterns of activity or learned [behavior] occur because one sensation response is associated with another."[10] In other words, how we determine if an experience is happy or hurtful will be based on how that experience is emotionally associated to past experience of happiness or hurt.

Thus, if life's experiences are shaped by emotional perceptions of happiness or hurt, then what does a life pursuant to discipleship in Christ look like when that life is asked to "pick up it's cross?" And if we must pick up our crosses and pick them up daily, then what will our life's journey consist of? Lastly, how will associations to life's experienced hurtful hardships of the past affect the healthy development of our present discipleship?

---

[10] May, Gerald G. *Addictions and Grace*. New York: HarperCollins, 1988, p. 55.

With these questions in mind, let us take a quick look at how Jesus dealt with a similar issue.

Luke 9.57–62, speaks of three supposed followers of Jesus. We are told that the first of these three was a scribe, a man allegedly skilled in the art of interpretation of the Scripture. As we soon learn, this scribe decided to undergo Jesus' tutelage. Yet, when this man pronounces to Jesus, "Teacher, I will follow you wherever you go." Jesus' response was not one of affirmation but seemingly of discouragement. "Foxes have dens, birds have nest, but the Son of Man has no place to rest His head." Was Jesus denying this man fellowship by discouraging him from following? Quite the contrary, Jesus was forecasting the discomforts that may come with being a disciple.

The second supposed follower of Jesus is more interesting than our first. Unlike our scribe, this one is identified as a actual *disciple*. To be clear, our second supposed follower did not make a declaration to follow Jesus. This man was already *following* Jesus. Yet, he chooses this moment to give Jesus this condition, "Let me go bury my father, first." Jesus' reply is legendary. "Let the dead bury their own dead."

Did Jesus just insult this man's father? Was Jesus conveying a tyrannical monarchist leader that shoves His followers into ultimatums of blind subservience? This, too, was not the case. Jesus was not referring to the father as dead but to the disciple as *not* willing to pursue *life.* However, it is Jesus' reply to our third supposed follower that gives us the most succinct understanding here.

Our third supposed follower (and the saddest, in my opinion), was a man Jesus *personally* invites to be His disciple. However, this alleged follower replies, "let me go home first..." In response, Jesus states, "No one who puts his hand to the plow and looks back is fit for the Kingdom of God." Though, this exchange appears to be similar to Jesus conversation with the second supposed follower, they are contrastingly different.

The second supposed follower was seeking a livelihood engrossed in security. Do not forget, this "disciple" had just heard Jesus tell the scribe that the Son of Man had no place to rest His head. Thus, this supposed disciple's motivation was solely based on seeking a loophole from the discomforts of discipleship.

Also, if you consider the nuances found in Jesus' dialogue with the second supposed "follower," there was an awaited inheritance for him to gain as a result of his father's death. Therefore, Jesus' remarks were simply to say, "you're choosing to inherit the dead instead of inheriting life." The author of Hebrews provides us with a perfect comparison to this matter. "Esau, sold his birth-right in exchange for one meal. For you know that later, when he wanted to inherit the blessing, he was rejected because he didn't find any oppor-tunity for repentance, though he sought it with tears."[11] No one of us can serve two masters. And this supposed follower was seeking the secu-rity of a fixed livelihood. Our third supposed fol-lower was not.

Note: Christ saw this would be follower's heart. We know this from the response Jesus chooses to open up their dialogue with... "Follow me." Christ saw in this man the potential to be a disciple and true "follower." However, this supposed follower struggled with separation anxiety.

Unwilling to part from his family, he disqual-ified himself from his discipleship. He associ-ated following Jesus' will with losing his family. Unwilling to depart from his family, this would-be disciple willingly parts from Christ. In a meta-physical reality, this man had not understood that Christ was not asking him to detach from his family but to cleave onto God, as a wife cleaves onto her husband.

Moreover, the nuance behind the statement, "he who puts his hand to the plow..." clearly implies

---

[11]   Holy Bible. Hebrews 12.16-17.

that this man had the constitution to do the work. However, he lacked the fortitude to maintain his relationship to God in its proper place. Again, this was not Jesus forcing this man to disown His family, this was Jesus disclosing the type of hardships that His followers would face, and in this instance, a period is separation.

John 1.14 describes Jesus as being full of Grace and Truth. Jesus gracefully explains the truth but...

> *Jesus never gives a false impression to His disciples about the events they will experience throughout their discipleship.*

Discipleship in Christ does and *will* include experienced events of hurt. Contrary to popular belief, we must experience times of suffering as it is said in 1 Peter 5.10. However, in that same verse God promises to personally confirm, restore, strengthen and establish us.

Looking into Philippians 3.10, we find a shiny silver lining to our suffrage. *"... to experience the power of His [Christ's] resurrection, to share in His suffering, and to be like Him in His Death."*[12] Experiencing Christ's *power* is in direct correlation to our *sharing* in His *suffering.* As much as, *being*

---

[12] Ibid., Philippians 3.10.

like Him includes the *likeness* of His *death*. Simply put, resurrection implies dying, and putting to death any and everything that is not in accordance to Christ's likeness.

Because the nature of associationism is to relate emotional responses of happiness or hurtful to past experiences perceived as similar to the current experience, Holy Spirit will put us into, what I like to call, the "pit stops" of life.

The Pit Stops

Emotions are associated with bodily reactions activated by the brain. Our emotions are physical reactions to outward stimuli. Consequently, our emotions can be shaped by our experiences. Our feelings, on the other hand, are the conscious experiences of emotional reactions. It is our feelings that actually perceive what we are experiencing emotionally.[13]

John 14.26 tells us, "the Counselor, the Holy Spirit —the Father will send Him in My name—will teach you all things and remind you of everything

---

[13]   Angers, Laura. Feelings V. Emotions: Is there A Difference Between Them?, 2020. 28 Aug. 2020 <http://www.betterhelp.com/advice/general/inns-vs-emotions-is-there-a-difference-between-them/

I have told you."[14] Thus, it is part of Holy Spirit's work as the Counselor in our lives to help us identify areas of emotional association in order to recognize patterns of behavior needing change. However, this requires us to develop appropriate responses to the feelings associated with our old nature.

Paul states in Ephesians 4:22-24, "You took off your former way of life, the old self that is corrupted by deceitful desires; you are being renewed in the spirit of your minds; you put on the new self, the one created according to God's likeness in righteousness and purity of the truth."[15]

As previously stated, our emotions are the instinctive physical reactions to perceived happiness or hurt that have been shaped by our life experiences. Our emotions are interwoven into, what Paul is referring to as, the old self that is "corrupted by deceitful desires." Remember, our emotions are shaped by our life experiences and the traditions of truth or lies to which we have been exposed. And, if our emotions are shaped, our emotions can also be manipulated. Thus, if not properly reshaped and guarded, our

---

[14] Holy Bible. John 14.26-27.

[15] Ibid., Ephesians 4.22-24.

emotions become doorways that allow the enemy to tempt us.

Take, for instance, Jesus. After He was baptized, Scripture tells us that He was led by the Holy Spirit into the wilderness to be tempted by Satan for forty days and nights. After Christ reached His fortieth day, Jesus feels hungry. Satan, finding opportunity, seeks to tempt our Lord by challenging Him to turn stone into bread. Jesus' reply was, "Man must not live on bread alone but on every word that comes from the mouth of God."[16]

Observe, Satan seeks to tempt Jesus by evoking an emotion. Satan's challenge to prove the veracity of Christ's Sonship was an attempt to cause Jesus to react emotionally and act outside of God's will. Jesus, being God, could have most certainly turned stone to bread. However, had Christ done so, God would have been proven to be flawed. Had Christ repurposed God's intended plan for His creation by turning stone into bread, He would have proven God to be uncertain and His word untrustworthy. By turning stone into bread, He would have proven God to be a liar and caused God to go against His own word. And if God's word would have been open for alteration, God's word would have been rendered insufficient. Turning

---

[16]   Ibid., Matthew 4.4.

stone into bread would have meant that what God has spoken into existence could be changed, what God has spoken could be revised, what God has spoken could be repurposed, and what God has spoken could be redefined.

Christ, on the other hand, does not react emotionally. Instead, He allows Himself to form feelings informed by Truth in accordance to His own word. "Man must not live on bread alone but on every word that comes from the mouth of God."

Translation: the way we live must not be based on our emotional drives. our emotional drives must be based on every way God tells us to feel about our living.

In their book, "Tough Faith," authors Janet and Craig Parshall eloquently explain,

> *"Our emotional life and physical circumstances are behind everything else because they cannot be relied upon to determine the direction of our faith. Instead, feelings are the byproduct of our spiritual walks. If this were not true, when we experience a sterile "desert" phase emotionally, the truth of Scripture would cease to be true. When we make*

> *our inward spiritual feelings the guide for all things, our Christian theology begins to look more like a rollercoaster of how we feel about Him."*[17]

Let us consider, again, what Ephesians 4.23 tells us. By the renewing of the *spirit* of our mind, the old self that is corrupted is being removed. The *spirit* of our mind is the very essence that brings forth life into our thoughts. Similarly, feelings are the consciousness of our emotions. Feelings bring perception to our emotions. Thus, feelings that have been surrendered to Holy Spirit bring proper perspective to our emotions.

It is for this reason Paul calls for the renewing of the *spirt* of our minds. Renewing the spirit of our minds produces renewed thoughts, and renewed thought produce renewed feelings. Furthermore, without renewed feelings we cannot act in renewed behavior. The way we think affects the way we feel, and the way we feel influences the way we act.

Let us recall one last thing. Jesus was led to be tempted for forty days and nights by none other than Holy Spirit. Consequently, there are times where we are led into trials by Holy Spirit. But it

---

[17] Parshall, Janet and Craig, Tough Faith. Oregon: Harvest House. 1990., p.84

is in this irony that we find Holy Spirit's commitment to our success. The pit stops He directs us to are always purposed with experiences that are filled with associations of our past so that He can reshape, restructure, repurpose our feelings and perceived emotions to their truthful and trustworthy intendedness.

Similar to NASCAR, the pit stops are the sections designated for us during the race to pull over, be serviced, and receive replacement parts. Similarly, our pit stops serve to provide us with necessary service to tend to the damaged parts we have incurred along the race. And it is in the pit stops that our damaged parts are replaced with newer parts to complete the journey and end strong.

Yet, none of this is possible without the confrontation between what is being actualized to what God is intending. Consequently, what results from these confrontations are the ebbs and flows between the flesh and the Spirit that is highlighted in Romans chapter seven.

These ebbs and flows shape our reality as disciples of Christ.

Chapter 2

THE CROSSROADS

. . . .

I t had only been a few months into my new position when news of change arose around the
office. These arbitrary changes resulted in many
people undergoing lay-offs. I was one of the few
included in this number. This change blindsided
the entire ministry team because we all were
beginning to establish growth and momentum.
The direction we appeared to be heading towards
seemed better than they actually were. Moreover,
our constituents had started to feed off of the
enthusiasm and enjoyment the team. I, personally, was baffled by how quickly I had become
displaced.

Over the next few days, my sleep became
affected and soon after, I began to project hurtful
feelings towards those closest to me. The per-
plexity of this unforeseen scenario was sending
me down a path of complete apathy and anger.

After all, I had left everything. I had altered my life to accommodate the needs of this ministry. Now, I was being left with nothing.

For several days my mind was a flutter with unpredictability, and I could not think clearly. So, in a moment of overwhelming indecisiveness, I forced myself to make one decision. I decided to go for a walk.

It was a solemn evening. The night's air was cool and crisp. The dark canopy of the universe seemed to envelope me into a thoughtful drifting of introspective meditation. The ambient atmosphere massaged the spring night with a gentle touch of serenity. When suddenly, I found myself immersed in what appeared to be a cathartic discourse of hostility towards God. My walk down the path was unlike any of my previous walks, in that, it was the first time since my arrival at Somerset that I felt stranded and without any direction.

I started to barter with God in an effort to alleviate my distress. I did not know it then, but even when the path seems without a direction, the direction is still along the path. Psalm 56:8 tells us, "You Yourself [God] have recorded my wanderings. Put my tears in Your bottle. Are they not in Your records?"[18] With Christ, we are never left stranded and in wandering.

Emotions will supersede your intelligence if you allow it. And, I was downward spiraling through a helix of moods. "But, why?" I bellowed with the carnivorous cry of a lone wolf by the moon night. Then the Spirit reminded me, "...All things work together for good for those who love God, who are called according to his purpose, because those whom he foreknew he also predestined to be conformed to the image of his Son..."[19]

As I meditated on these words, the Spirit led me into a deep discovery of what it means to be called in accordance to conformity to the image of Christ. All things work together according to his purpose and *to be conformed* to His image**.**

Being called in "Accordance" is to be in consistency with the process of becoming more like Christ.

In other words, the Holy Spirit is deliberate about forming us in the sameness and likeness of who we are to Christ. Moreover, the Holy Spirit will work "all things" to His advantage for the

---

[18] Holy Bible. Psalm 56.8.

[19] Ibid., Romans 8.28-29.

purpose of changing that which is *not* in congruence with Christ.

Although God's plans are for our good, He will occasionally cause *all things* – even the bad – to temporarily occur for the permanent good He is producing inside us. In some awkward ideality of reality, even the bad things that may happen to us in this life God sees as being useful for shaping us into his image. This is what James is pronouncing when he says, "Consider it '*all*' joy when you fall into '*all*' trials."[20]

This leads me to the next point. To be *conformed* to Christ's image is *not* to assume that Christ places a demand for us to assimilate to other Christians. In contrast, conformity in Christ embraces how fearful, wonderful, and *distinct* we are as it is in regard to *how He desires* us to be. Unlike assimilation that makes demands to be absorbed, consumed, engrossed, fused, preoccupied, or saturated by how everyone else appears, the Holy Trinity speaks clearly to the sacredness and sacrosanctity that God reveres in the distinction He created us in.

God the Father, God the Son, and God the Holy Spirit are one and the same. Yet, God the Father is of a distinct personality from God the Son, just

---

[20]   Ibid., James 1.2.

as God the Son is of a distinct personality from God the Holy Spirit. Still, they are one and the same. They all speak for one another, point to one another, and give glory to each other. These distinctions are by extension *virtuous* and glorifying to God. To best sum up the virtuousness that is in distinctiveness, we need look at 1 Corinthians 12. 14-20.

> *"For in fact the body is not a single member, but many. If the foot says, "Since I am not a hand, I am not part of the body," it does not lose its membership in the body because of that. And if the ear says, "Since I am not an eye, I am not part of the body," it does not lose its membership in the body because of that. If the whole body were an eye, what part would do the hearing? If the whole were an ear, what part would exercise the sense of smell? But as a matter of fact, God has placed each of the members in the body just as He decided. If they were all the same member, where would the body be? So now there are many members, but one body."*[21]

---

[21] Ibid., 1 Corinthians 12. 14-20.

The distinctiveness of the body to its body parts gives us a clear delineation of how Christ views us as individuals who are many but part of a whole. Being conformed to Christ is in direct relation to who we were made to be, how we have been made to function, and the way we are characteristically. Still, who we are, how we have been made, and what is characteristic of us needs to conform to who Christ is, how Christ is, and what is characteristic of Christ.

Notice how Romans 8.28 and 29 are in harmony with each other. Verse 28 calls for us to be *called in accordance*, while verse 29 follows up with our *conformity to Christ*. Accordance and conformity are consistent with one another. Simply put, *all things* are made *in accordance* with our *conformity* to the *character* of Christ.

> **Hence, the loss of my position served to only reveal a quality in me that was inconsistent with Christ's character and the person Christ had truly intended for me to be.**

The assurance that results in the Holy Spirit started to rest upon my heart. Realizing that I had tarried on this path longer than usual, I decided to make my way back to the parsonage. I had never walked along the red road at night, and I could barely make out the path. Still, I felt confident enough to walk along the way since I had walked this walkway enough times. Little did I realize that the path possessed crossing paths and I had soon found myself lost.

Assurance quickly became replaced with anxiety. My thoughts shifted into a survivors instinct that immediately flooded my mind with varying degrees of escape. But the darkness seemed to engulf my surroundings and I no longer possessed the confidence of moving forward. I then grew weary and made another decision. I decided to just stop moving. Having paused in that moment, I did what any person at a point of desperation would do. I cried out to the Lord.

In that instant I felt God hear me. Holy Spirit then instructed, "Go back to where it was from where you started." As I proceeded to go back from where I started, Holy Spirit began to remove the covering over my eyes and helped me realize my straight path was actually a crossroad. In each step back in the direction I came from, Holy Spirit revealed the areas of my life needing exposure that had for so long been held in undisclosed truth. Holy Spirit then revealed to me He was never moving me forward. He had always intended to have me double back.

**The journey forward sometimes requires
us to go backward, first.**

My first error was to assume that I had arrived
at a good place and had settle on the idea that I
met my destination. Instead, I should have realized that I was still along the path of my journey.
There is a temptation that comes with feeling good
or better about where you are in life. The temptation is to become settled on the idea that your
destination is met. As a result, we become com-
placent and demotivated to take further action.

Moving towards your destination requires
going forward in the direction of your destination.
However, moving forward means you have to take
new steps. It is easy to assume motion for moving.
It's even easier to assume moving as being synonymous with going forward. But moving forward
in life always possesses the nuance of new. Why?
Forward is ahead of you. Moving forward is always
symbolic of going to where you are not... yet.

My second mistake was failing to remember
the nature of the Holy Spirit's work in our lives.
It is the nature of Holy Spirit working in our lives
to walk us through *all things;* to bring *all things in
accordance* to *conformity* of *Christ,* and cause *all
things* to function *characteristically* to *Christ.* Thus,
when there are areas in our lives that are found

not in accordance with Christ, are not conformed to Christ, and or differ from the character of Christ, it is the responsibility of Holy Spirit to yield to the area of disconformity and forge its tailoring.

God will not allow us to *fail forward.* God is not into "social promotions." He relishes individual success. Consequently, the Holy Spirit will keep walking us through our failure until our failure becomes our success. After all, He is the God of our *success*, not our failure!

My third error during this season of my life was to assume that I had already been fully conformed to Christ's image. As I had mentioned earlier, the loss of my position served to reveal inconsistencies in my character. I asked myself, "What was it about my position with this ministry that I had emotional attachments to?" As my mind drifted back and forth in this quandary of query, guilt worked itself into the corridors of my soul. "Where is your faith?", I argued. "What man of God questions God?" The voice of self-accusation cracked its whip.

In a moment of personal self-loathing, I became paralyzed with fear. My emotional stairway began stepping downward toward a darkened abyss. Then, Holy Spirit broke into a state of assertive posturing. "Come let us reason together, says the

Lord: though your sins are like scarlet, they shall be as white as snow."[22]

> *Good questions will get you great answers. And, in the context of doubt, God builds faith. Thus, when you trust God even in your faithlessness, God shows himself always faithful.*

My journey was now taking a "right" turn but the road was about to get a bit rocky.

---

[22] Ibid., Isaiah 1.18.

Chapter 3

TROUBLED TERRAIN

. . . .

That which is born of the flesh, remains in the flesh.[23] That which is born of the flesh remains at the base level of the flesh: sensory, emotional, sporadic, and lead by the primordial appetites lingering in the unregenerate soul. Ironically, this list of carnal givens is also a depiction of how some of us describe our encounter with Holy Spirit. Some of us even dare to refer to the leading of Holy Spirit as "streams of consciousness."

This makes me wonder whether or not what we consider to be "Spirit-led" is correct or mistaken. Again, what is of the flesh is of the flesh. Therefore, it is a mistake to assume our sensory driven sporadic notions of emotional fervor are perfect indicators for a "Spirit-led" experience. Moreover, "streams of consciousness" are nothing

---

[23] Ibid., John 3.6.

more than numerous amounts of thoughts and emotions passing through the individual mind spontaneously, impulsively, and involuntary. These are uncharacteristic of the Holy Spirit. In contrast, the Holy Spirit acts as follows:

> *The Holy Spirit loves order, and He therefore sets our powers and faculties in due places, giving the highest room to those spiritual faculties which link us with the great King; let us not disturb the divine arrangement, but ask for grace that we may keep under our body and bring it into subjection, we were not new created to allow our passions to rule over us..."*[24]

This falls in line with what is stated in Scripture, "the spirit of the prophets are subject to the prophets."[25] Thus, for those of us who reference this verse as the qualifier for intermittent forms of ecstatic sensations as signs of Holy Spirit, please allow me to suggest the following. The term "spirit" as it is used in this verse is not to be confused with the Spirit of Holy Spirit.

---

[24] Spurgeon, Charles, Morning and Evening.

[25] Holy Bible., 1 Corinthians 14.23.

"Spirit," here, refers to the soul of the individual person operating within a specific gift. And it is in the ability of the said individual to come into compliance with the orderly manner in which Holy Spirit will operate. Furthermore, it is important for us to recognize the nuance of the text and how it implicitly calls out for clarity of the senses, control of the emotions, and continuity in how the Spirit of God moves. The implication behind the statement "subject to the prophets" is a clear indication for the spirit of the person remaining in full mastery of the person. As a result of being under inspiration of the Holy Spirit, one still possesses their natural facilities, faculties, and functions of their own behavior. God does not possess, only Satan is possessive. God seeks participation. Unlike Satan, God wants a partner not a puppet.

Being born of the Spirit is a transformation of the old sensory driven, emotional lead, and sporadic nature into a new nature of order, soundness of mind, and self-control.

What is born of the Spirit transcends the fundamental forbearance of the flesh and allows us to perceive the effects of the Spirit within us by developing, forming, shaping, and reforming our passions, with a greater understanding of the

Holy Spirit's guided spiritedness towards Christ-centered virtues. The virtues the Holy Spirit endeavors to develop in us are virtues He aspires to be developed in three areas of our being: our spirits, our souls, and our bodies.

We are made in God's image and likeness. Thus, we are a trinity in similar manner that God is a trinity. God is Father, Son, and Holy Spirit. We are spirit, soul, and body. Therefore, when we become born again, the Holy Spirit transposes our spirit with His own Spirit, transforms our souls in the likeness of His thoughts and feelings, and as a result the body acts upon the new behavior that is in reflection of the Spirit's conduct. Simply put, being born again needs to occur in three spheres. Our spirit's need to be born again, our souls need to be born again, and our bodies need to be born again.

As I have previously stated, we are a trinity in similar manner to God. We are spirit, soul, and body. And by extension, the three are one. Therefore, a transformed spirit shapes a transformed soul, and a transformed soul informs a transformed body.

Remember Ephesians 4.22, we... "lay aside the old self, which is being corrupted in accordance with the lusts of deceit, and that you be *renewed in the spirit of your mind*, and put on the new self, which in the likeness of God..." Let me take this time to tie these two thoughts together.

At the point of our belief within our heart and confession with our mouth that Jesus Christ is Lord and Savior, Holy Spirit identifies us as His own. As Jesus explained to Nicodemus, we are now born of the Spirit. Thus, our spirit is immediately saved. However, the soul, the part of our humanity that contains our consciousness, the substance of thoughts, and the essence of our feelings, begins to experience the transforming work of sanctification through the indwelling of Holy Spirit. And as our thoughts and feelings become *transformed*, our behavior immediately follows in conformity.

Did you catch the pattern? Did you take notice how Holy Spirit repeatedly recapitulates who we are predestined to be in accordance to the image we are conforming to? Again, we are a trinity in a similar manner to God's triune person.

Much simpler, our thinking leads our feelings, and feelings lead our behavior. Thus, it is in the light of this truth that Holy Spirit is able to point out unshakable realities that have shaped our mental perceptions keeping us from a proper action. Consequently, this molding and shaping does, at times, require us to walk through some troubled terrain.

Troubled Terrain

Like most inner-city minority males, I had grown up in a broken family with an absentee father. Consequent to my father's drug use, my mother, my sister, and I were homeless for two years. The trauma would prove to have great impact on much of the way I perceived, believed, and behaved towards people...including God. However, these perceptions would remain dormant until the winter of 2003.

He was a ministry leader, an elder of my church, and he was said to be *"Prophetic."* The last point is important because the church I was attending during this time of my life was a church of sound doctrine and a church of integrity. Thus, when he sought me out and said to me, "Raymond, the Holy Spirit has lead me to speak to you." I did not hesitate to agree to meet with him.

Looking back, I should have read the signs. The Scriptures warn us to "test every kind of spirit."[26] However, I was an immature Christian, naive to Scriptural truth in order to see things for what they were. But I was also desperate. And desperate people are never picky. Thus, I accepted his invitation.

---

[26] Ibid., 1 John 4.1.

I remember the excitement I felt the day he called me to schedule an appointment for counseling. I was elated. I thought to myself, "Surely, I will get some clarity. God speaks through him!" In my mind, the experience with an elder would be like a parishioner receiving the Holy Eucharist from the hand of the priest. In my mind, I was about to encounter God manifest. No one had warned me to be very careful of how we idolize others.

Fear and trembling combined with fervor and anticipation blended in my system producing higher levels of dopamine that pumped through my veins like a jackhammer to concrete as I drew closer and closer to my meeting time. The winter breeze helped to tether the intense amount of adrenaline overheating my anxiousness body.

Approaching my destination, I could remember the clamorous sounds of the mid-town traffic appearing tapered and agreeable. Walking vigorously through the concrete terrain, I could see the city skyline laying in front of me dressed in an overcoat of cerulean smudged with swashes of white that steered around the great Titan hordes of stone and mortar. My nostrils filled with the scent of overcooked meat and sweetened edible kernels. Yet, none of these things could deter me from reaching the end point of my journey. Finally, I arrived at the front door of his apartment building.

As I stood in front of the main entrance, I struggled to press my finger on his apartment button that alerts him of my arrival. For those short few seconds, I began to consider the idea of turning back and going home. However, I had already come a long way and thought I would later regret ever not knowing what encounter I would experience with God should I decide to leave. I could not have been more wrong.

As I pressed the buzzer, the door unlocks and as I entered into the elder's apartment building I became grafted into a surreal existence. The mind is a very powerful machine able to fabricate and authenticate perceptible phenomenon with absolute certainties, only to deceive oneself into believing they are experiencing realities they are not.

Thus, my mind improvised an alternate dimension where I crossed over the threshing of a time rift that plunged me into a parallel reality of my own. My emotions started to get the better of me. I began to imagine myself being transported into a seraphic dwelling where I was too corrupt to enter. So, I began to pray a prayer of repentance hoping that I could be covered under mercy's generous dismissal for any unspoken transgressions.

Gingerly, I approached his apartment doorway when I heard the door latch unlock. The door's slow and pendulous swing was like a curtain crawling left stage to introduce its audience to the main character of a play. There he stood, arms spread open, smiling with great cheer, and jovial over my arrival.

Entering his apartment, my ears became aware of the low intonation of worshipers harmonizing over the pre-recorded release of praises. His home smelt of lightly fragrant incense and potpourri. Everything in this living space was aesthetically inviting and unassuming.

As he prompted my advance, the elder began to ask why I thought he would invite me over. "For spiritual counseling and prayer," I replied. In reciprocity, he explains, "No, Raymond, there is more." His gaze then shifted to a trace-like state completely absent to the surrounding stimuli. He proceeded to tell me, "The spirit tells me you have a carnal spirit oppressing you." He further explained that in order for me to be truly free, I would need to undergo a method of deliverance specifically designed for such a condition. He then led me to two accounts in the Bible.

He showed me Matthew 17.21: "this kind does not come out except by prayer." Then, pointing to Isaiah 20.20, he explained "God demanded Isaiah to walk around naked and barefoot for three years as a symbol of obedience to God." Hence

I, too, had to prepare to follow this same level of extreme obedience in order to receive deliverance from God. Blindly, foolishly, I desperately agreed to participate. From this point on, I was led into a spiritual ritual of "cleansing," as he called it.

This ritual cleansing required me to relieve myself of "a carnal seed." In other words, I would have to palliate male emission into a handkerchief for me to be free of this "corrupt seed." I agreed and the ritual cleansing began. As the ritual proceeded, I found myself half-conscious and non-cognizant of my occurrences. Several hours later I found myself kneeled over, in my mother's lap, wrapped up in my sister's arms, crying tears of great distress because of the nightmare I just woke up from.

Behind the Dark Curtain

Consequently, I have no memories to account for the several hours between my "ritual cleansing" and my return home. What I can remember was the darkness I encountered during those hours. Terror cannot explain the evil and psychological torture I experienced as I walked behind the dark dimensional curtain of the dark spiritual world for those several hours.

Behind this curtain was a world veiled in dark shade and lurking shadows. The world appeared cloaked under smoke and soot. The eclipsed airspace kept people concealed under their silhouettes. And beyond the outlines of the dark shade, living shadows would come encircle themselves around me chanting menacing declarations of shame and humiliation.

These specters would whisper over one another fighting to be heard. "You belong to us, now." They would shriek. "You will never escape your fate of hell." They provoked. "You are a child of the devil." They molested. Here, the spirit of fear made my acquaintance while I searched for light. Still, the most fretful feeling I had experienced amongst all of this was the feeling of a loss of hope.

It is strange to have to rely on the memories of others to get a clear picture of your life when you have no memories of your own. To be clear, I do not have any memories of leaving the elder's apartment. I do not have any memories of how I got home. I do not have any memories of my mother finding me peeling the top layers of my skin off my arms while I sat curled up in the corner of the bathtub. I do not have any memories of running through the apartment to evade my mother and sister touch because it felt like burning. Nor do I have any memories of the following events which lead to my mother and sister falling into full blown spiritual battle for my soul. What I do remember, however, was the room becoming filled with my cries for Jesus to come and help me, seeing the darkness, the murkiness of the shadows, and the cloaked smokey soot evaporate from my sight into several different directions.

For the next couple of months, my life would experience testing and uneasiness. I could not sleep with the lights out or with the door closed. The few times I attempted to do so, my mind would race and wander into the memories of that darkened world. Shadows still appeared to take form and draw close to me. Moreover, these fear tactics began to cause a state of paranoia and anxiety in me that stimulated all kinds of dissuading towards assurance in the deliverance found in Christ.

For those two months I had isolated myself from others. The paranoia increased. "Paranoid people don't get better on their own. You can't just tell them to "change their thinking." This is an isolated assignment, and isolation is the problem."[27] Thus, my isolation stirred in me all sorts of obsessive ideas in an attempt to rationalize my pain.

I began to debating with myself. "Should I expose this event to my church leadership." I started thinking. "I want justice for myself. I feel exploited, preyed upon, and taken advantage of."

---

[27]   Cloud, Dr. Henry. Changes that Heal. Michigan: ZondervanPublishing. 1992., p71.

I continued. The lingering thought brewed into a sense of moral responsibility to make sure this would not happen to another person. However, each time I would begin to build the courage to do so, the spirit of fear would grab hold of my ear and begin to ask, "Who would you tell? How will they receive this news? Who will take you seriously, Ray? Who do you think you are? You think your word will mean anything to them? How so you think they are going to look at you after finding out what you did?"

The questions continued to circulate in my mind to the point of nausea. I had felt myself slipping into listlessness. One day, my mother comforts me by telling me, "Ray, God did not give us a spirit of fear!" And with those resonating words, I was able gain the courage to face these issues even if it meant I had to do it... afraid. I finally broke silence.

It is unfortunate for me to tell you that I did not receive empathy, great support, and applause for my courage to speak out. Compared to my stint behind the dark curtain, my experience with my fellow brothers and sisters was much more hurtful.

"How *stupid of you... You're so foolish...* Now that was *dumb...*" were the statements I received. I was even laughed at and joked about. The humiliation I experienced from brothers and sisters from the church made me question the validity Christianity. I felt betrayed. Instead of empathy, the church community had now made me feel like the church social pariah.

This experience had risen old memories of my years of homeless. Moreover, it had awoken dormant feelings of rejection I had developed during those childhood years. The feeling of rebellion began to creep in, and I now found myself pushing the church away completely.

The several months that followed were a skirmish with doubts about religion and the integrity of the church. I had soon found myself alone, engaged in intense studies, and researching the Scriptures. I had hoped that I would find an answer that could satiate my discomfort. However, I grew weary and one evening, in frustration, launched my bible across my room,.

Sitting in a corner of my room with guilt arising for tossing my bible, I asked myself, "Why?" It's just a book." "No, it is not!" I heard Holy Spirit whisper in my ear. "In it is *the* way, *the* truth, and *the* life set for you, Ray. So, pick it back up and open to Genesis 39.21 and read!"

"But, the Lord was with Joseph in prison."

Tears formed at the inner corners of my eyes as I began to feel His presence upon me, wrapping me into His warm embrace and comforting me. As the Spirit reminded me of each event of Joseph's experience, I can feel healing occur in those parts of my soul that long been re-traumatized. At this moment I experienced God's faithfulness and His ability to complete the good He starts. Out of this traumatic experience, God was able to pour a drive in me that hinged on one fact. *He loved me!*

From this point on, I would endeavor to know God, Christ, and Holy Spirit, by their characteristics, by their nature, and by their personality. It was at this point in my life that I endeavored to know the Scriptures in a way that would never leave me to be harmed or to cause harm.

Chapter 4

QUICKSAND

. . . .

N o one of us is a single thing. Because Adam and Eve ate from the tree of Knowledge of Good and Evil, we are troubled with two inter-woven characteristics within our human nature... good and evil. All of our good is intertwined with all of our evil. This interweaving of our good and evil can be best described as "Selfishness" or a desire for "Self." A desire for "Self" can be viewed on two levels which mirror each other from its polar opposite.

For example, vanity's mirror opposite is dif-fidence. Although they both appear contrary to one another, they both share a common motive; a need for attention. Another example of this is longing for "Self" can be seen in anger. Anger is a strong feeling of discontent or dissatisfaction. In other words, "Self" desires to be satisfied. In contrast, depression is anger inverted. Where anger demands to express discontent outwardly, depression declares to express its discontent inwardly. Anger explodes, its equal opposite depression, implodes. Here is one more example to help hone in on this point of the interweaving of good and evil within our "Self."

Humility is commonly mistaken for the opposite of Pride. However, pride's opposite is actually asceticism. Consider what pride calls for: self-adoration, the delighting of self, self-glorification, and egotism. Asceticism places the demand on self-denial, the forbidding of self, self-abasement, and modesty. At face value, asceticism appears pious, virtuous, and even a righteous byproduct. Yet, asceticism is nothing more than sanctimonious and pietistic if it's only dedicated to reforming a troublesome area of our life. Asceticism should not be confused with consecration. Consecration is when we dedicate our struggle through compliance to God's transforming work in us.[28] In contrast, asceticism is dedicating ourselves to the actual struggle.

Christ provides us with this distinction between asceticism and consecration when speaking of the hypocrisy of the pharisees as a cup that was cleaned on the *OUTSIDE* but still filthy on the inside.

---

[28] May, Gerald, p. 150.

Jesus explicitly states, "in the same way, on the outside you *seem* righteous to people, but inside you are full of hypocrisy and lawlessness."[29] As you can see, outside of the consecration of our lives towards the new nature found in being born-again, all that is good in us will always be advised by all that is evil or "selfish" in us.

It is the power of inherent sinful selfishness that will always be the impetus that sparks our desire towards our own self-seeking, self-relying, self-gratifying, and self-assurances. It is true that we are all generally good. Yet, we are also inherently evil. It is the powers of "Self" that will always cause us to compromise that part of us that is considered good with a selfish intent. For this very reason, being born-again through faith in Jesus is necessary. Through Jesus Christ, we are not made more good or less evil. Through Jesus we become *Holy*.

The Good and Evil "Self"

Our humanity locks us into a dichotomy of truth. Dr. Henry Cloud explains the dichotomy this way...

> *"The world around us is good and bad. The people around us are good and bad. We*

---

[29] Holy Bible, Matthew 23.28.

are good and bad. Our natural tendency is to try and resolve the problem of good and evil by keeping the good and the bad separate. We want, by nature, to experience the good me, the good other, and the good world as "all good." To do this, we see the bad me, the bad other, and the bad world as "all bad." This creates a split in our experience of ourselves, others, and the world around us–a split that is not based on reality and cannot stand the test of time and real life."[30]

We are simultaneously intelligent and foolish, strong and weak, spirit and flesh. Thus, it is in this dichotomy that we will find our greatest battles. This battle is the "...splitting of the wills in two, one part desiring freedom and the other desiring only to continue in [sinful] behavior."[31] In this battle of opposites, our reality becomes convoluted, disturbed, and entangled. This is why it is important to discern the side of truth (or lie) we are battling from.

To be clear, truth is exclusive. Truth can never be what is real and unreal at the same time. To define one thing to be true means to define

---

[30] Cloud, Henry, p. 216.

[31] May, Gerald, p. 42.

everything contrary to that one thing as *not* true. Truth cannot be found without distinction. Thus, to properly define truth for ourselves, we must appreciate both the fearful wonderful us and the terribly awful us as a whole and not as two separated beings.

On that account, when I say it is important to discern the side of the truth we are battling from, I am asking if the lens of truth you choose to distinguish the accuracy of correctness and rightness is truly in according with the Spirit of the Lord, or are you distinguishing truth according to our own personal faculties with the flesh. "Truth is what is real; it describes how things really are. Truth is the structural aspect of God's character. God's truth leads us to what is real, to what is accurate."[32] Therefore, truth outside of the context of truth that is found in Jesus Christ will, by extension, keep us locked in a perception of truth that is rooted in a lie.

The dichotomy of our humanity tends to trick us into deceiving ourselves with all sorts of insidious tricks and strategies. The flesh's single most purpose is to keep our carnal behavior continuing. It is these same personal faculties we are told in Colossians 3:5 to, "put to death..."[33]

---

[32] Cloud, Henry, p.7.

[33] Holy Bible, Colossians 3.5.

The flesh is the part of our human dichotomy that Scripture distinguishes as "*earthly*" in nature. A common error made amongst us is to identify our battles with such things as sexual immorality, impurity, lust, evil desires, and greed as only spiritual or even demonic ascendancies. This is not to be misunderstood as saying that our enemy and his angels are not actively attempting to influence these actions.

However, Colossians 2.15 reminds us that Christ "disarmed the rulers and authorities and disgraced them publicly..."[34] Simply put, the powers of Satan and his angels are limited to persuasion and not to the strength attributed to swaying our physical actions. Our behaviors are morally and practically our own responsibility.

The nature of our flesh is subtle. The nature of the flesh in its battle against the Spirit is to "naturally seek the least threatening way of trying to satisfy our ongoing for God, while still looking for loopholes..."[35] A good look at temptation and its relationship to our spiritual growth will show the battle between the flesh and the spirit as it relates to our human experience. "The Bible includes a wide variety of interpretations of temptation. In much

---

[34] Ibid., Colossians 2. 15.

[35] May, Gerald, p. 93.

of the New Testament, it is seen as the primary activity of the devil, *seduction*. At other times, temptation is viewed as part of the *human condition*."[36] Jesus, when asked to teach on prayer added this addendum to the invocation, "do not bring us into temptation..."[37] At the garden of Gethsemane, Jesus warns His trusted three to "stay awake and pray so that they would not enter into temptation..."[38] In both of these accounts, temptation is depicted as a doorway that we can enter. Our strength to overcome sin can be wielded through our willingness to flee temptation and avoid *entering* it's doors.

In retrospect, my experience in the ministry held an emotional association similar to my experience with the elder. They both were exploitations I encountered under the guise of being "Spirit Lead." Both events occurred during periods of my life where the efforts I was making were under the assumption they were steps towards my purpose in Christ. In both events I found myself exploited by those in the ministry. Both events caused me to endure forms of spiritual abuse and persecution.

Moreover, both events held nuances of refusal, rejection, and repudiation. These feelings were

[36] Ibid., p. 94.

[37] Holy Bible., Matt. 6.13.

[38] Ibid., Matt. 26.41.

associated to feelings of abandonment I experienced during my period of homelessness as a child. As a result, a desire to act in behavior that I had once used to anesthetize my suffering slowly started to loom. Before long, I began to regress and go into an emotional spiraling effect best known as being caught in the *Quicksand*.

Quicksand

There is a nature to quicksand that is systematically true of our human propensities. Quicksand is loose, wet, sandy topography that yields easily to pressure placed upon it. The pressure then causing the loose wet ground to swill down causing its surface to give way with no security for solid footing, creating the feeling of bottomlessness. Quicksand is also difficult to come out of. The more movement you make while in the quicksand, the more pressure you create. The pressure causes the surface to yield even quicker, causing a vacuum effect that produces suction. Ironically, one of the proper ways to deal with being caught in quicksand is to be as still as possible in order to slow up the process of submergence.

Contrastingly, Scripture tells us exactly what to do in times we find ourselves caught in the quicksand.

"Wait for the LORD; be strong, and let your heart be courageous. Wait for the LORD."

"We wait for the LORD; he is our help and shield."

"Be silent before the LORD and wait expectantly for him; do not be agitated by one who prospers in his way, by the person who carries out evil plans."

"Wait for the LORD and keep his way, and he will exalt you to inherit the land. You will watch when the wicked are destroyed."

"Now, Lord, what do I wait for? My hope is in you."[39]

The pressures of life can become overwhelmingly heavy. These pressures can produce feelings of unbearable weight we can no longer hold up. And when we encounter these time of great pressure in our lives, all our efforts appear to be of no avail. Simply put, we can appear to be sinking like in quicksand. Ironically, our inclination is not to use correct ways out of our times of desperation.

---

[39]   Ibid., Psalm 24.14, 33.20, 37.7, 34, 39.7.

Instead, we resort back to previous times of desperation as a reference for our survival.

My layoff generated feelings of rejection that triggered a spiritual discontent and hightened degrees of defensiveness. I began to act out in behaviors of spiritual rebellion. I became resistant, easily angered, and depressed. I desperately desired to keep myself from these feelings, even if for short stints of time. I found myself returning to the anesthetizing methods of drinking and pornography for relief from the pain.

I was submerged in the "Quicksand" without any medium for relief. More importantly, I was returning to the "Old Man" I put off during my conversion to Christ. "But, how?" I asked myself. "I thought that I was delivered, set free, liberated from such egregious behavior. Coincidentally, my sinful propensities were never removed, they were only in remission like a cancerous tumor that became reduced and rendered ineffective, but not gone. At the cross, our sinfulness becomes fruitless. While, sin is placed in remission, sinfulness it is not removed. Sin requires our will; *our sinfulness*. This is why Paul, in Romans eight, admonishes us not to walk in the flesh but in the Spirit. Furthermore, our walk with God is not a descending from the Spirit to the flesh but a transcending from the flesh to the Spirit.

1 Corinthians 15.46-49 explains it this way.

"However, the spiritual is not first, but the natural, then the spiritual. The first man was from the earth, a man of dust; the second man is from heaven. Like the man of dust, so are those who are of the dust; like the man of heaven, so are those who are of heaven. And just as we have borne the image of the man of dust, we will also bear the image of the man of heaven. "[40]

Here is our reality. We are sinners, *inherently*, *naturally*, and *willfully*. Therefore, our sinfulness coexists on three spheres, inherently or characteristic to our humanity, naturally or what is normal to our humanity, and willfully or what is intentional to our humanity. Let me provide you with further detail.

First, we are sinners inherently because of our forefather Adam. It is in our DNA. We have *inherited* a sinful quality. Secondly, we are sinners by nature. Upon the fall of humanity, all that is of nature became corrupted and, by extension, made to appeal to its nature which is now *naturally* sinful. Lastly, we all posses a power to choose that is free

---

[40] Ibid., 1 Corinthians 15. 46–49.

from coercion. Because Adam sinned willingly, we too, have a will to sin. Thus, we are sinful at *will*.

My sin had come out of remission and was starting to escalate. I found myself stuck and did not know what to do. Furthermore, I no longer had the ruddy red road. My ruddy road was replaced by an active street neighboring a highway. I felt myself stuck and desperately needing to get unstuck. With thoughts of impending danger growing and increasing weariness in my heart, I went out from my new apartment and I walked, only this time, I didn't have a red road to guide me.

I walked down avenues of unknown streets. I walked down sidewinding roads. I walked through asphalt walkways. I walked until I had no more road to walk. Reading the sign, "Dead End," I perceived this moment of my life as helplessness and without concession. Yet, God would not let me lose hope. "Ray, did you forget how I parted the Red Sea? I'm about to get you unstuck". Holy Spirit spoke. "Get ready... I do not deal with iniquity as I do with transgression," Holy Spirit resounded.

Chapter 5

GETTING UNSTUCK

. . . .

The reason why most of us become stuck in our sinfulness is because God does not deal with our iniquity as He deals with our transgressions. Provocative, isn't it? Well, let us puts eyes on several Scriptures.

> *Psalm 19.12–13: Who perceives his unintentional sins? Cleanse me from my hidden faults. Moreover, keep Your servant from willful sins; do not let them rule over me. Then I will be innocent and cleansed from blatant rebellion.*

> *Psalm 24.3–4: Who shall ascend the hill of the Lord? The one who has clean hands and a pure heart, who has not set his mind on what is false, and who has not sworn deceitfully.*

Psalm 32.1–2: Blessed is the one whose transgression is forgiven, whose sin is covered. Blessed is the man against whom the Lord counts no iniquity, and in whose spirit there is no deceit... I acknowledged my sin to you, and I did not cover my iniquity; I said, "I will confess my transgressions to the Lord," and you forgave the iniquity of my sin.

Ezekiel 37.23: They shall not defile themselves anymore with their idols and their detestable things, or with any of their transgressions. But I will save them from all the backsliding in which they have sinned, and will cleanse them; and they shall be my people, and I will be their God.

Did you know that there were two distinctions to sin? There is the sin of *Transgression* and there is the sin of *Iniquity*. The best way to describe these two sins is as follows:

Transgressions are sins that have transpired or transferred from thought to action. Transgressions are the behaviors that result from the sinful inclinations inherently within us. It is the behavior that

proceeds our feelings. Whereas, iniquity is the sin that is within us. Iniquity is the sinful way we perceive the world around us. It is the sin within. Thus, it is called..."In-iquity."

Observe, sins of transgression are identified as sins of transaction, actions, conduct, and ways of behaving. For example, Psalm 19 describes it as a *"willful sin."* When asking the rhetorical question of "who can ascend to the hill of the Lord?" The Psalmist explains, "those with *clean* hands, or those who have not *acted* on a transgression." Psalm 32 suggests that a person is blessed when their transgression is covered. Lastly, Ezekiel 37 suggests that transgressions defile. In other words, transgressions sully or soil the individual. In contrast, iniquity is of a more subtle quality.

Looking into these same Scriptures, you will see whimsical subtleties being revealed. For example, Psalm 19 describes transgression as a *"willful sin,"* iniquity is described as a *"hidden fault,"* where Psalm 24 calls for clean hands for our *transgressions*, it further calls for a *"pure heart"* for our *iniquity*. Psalm 32 declares a covering for transgressions but it also speaks of iniquity as *not* being counted against the person.

> **God deals with our iniquities quite**
> **different from our transgressions. Where**
> **God CLEANSES transgressions, God**
> **HEALS iniquity.**

Again, let us consider the whimsical subtleties being revealed through the Scriptures:

1. Psalm 19:12–13: "Who perceives his unintentional sins? Cleanse me from my hidden faults. Moreover, keep Your servant from willful sins; do not let them rule over me. Then I will be innocent and cleansed from blatant rebellion."
    1.1. "*Cleanse me from my hidden faults.*"
        1.1.1. Notice, CLEANSING is required from the HIDDEN FAULTS.
        1.1.2. In other words, the inner fault must be healed in order fort the outward errors to be corrected.
        1.1.3. Remember, the way we think will be the way we feel. And the way we feel, will inform the way we act or behave.
    1.2. "*Then I will be innocent and cleansed from blatant rebellion.*"
        1.2.1. Notice, INNOCENCE is the precursor to the cleansing from BLATANT REBELLION.
        1.2.2. In other words, my actions or behavior will not be corrected, "cleansed" even, unless

he interior of our soul, the part of us that gives breathe and life to our thinking and feelings is HEALED.

2. Psalm 24:3–4 (ESV): Who shall ascend the hill of the Lord? The one who has clean hands and a pure heart, who has not set his mind on what is false, and who has not sworn deceitfully.

   2.1.**"*The one who has clean hands and a pure heart...*"**

   2.1.1.Notice, CLEAN HANDS are the byproduct of a PURIFIED HEART.

   2.1.2.In other words, the heart has to undergo a purification process, a HEALING, in order for the actions of the HANDS to be CLEAN.

   2.2.**"*...who has not set his mind on what is false, and who has not sworn deceitfully.*"**

   2.2.1.Notice, it is the MIND that is resolved and concluded on the exclusivity of Truth and Truth only found in God, His Son, His Spirit, and the very Word of Truth declared by Him, that is a MIND that will not ACT by deceitfulness.

   2.2.2.In other words, we must be HEALED of deceptive ideas, ideologies, imaginations, interests, and inclinations in order to walk with PURITY OF HEART.

3. Psalm 32:1–2 (ESV): Blessed is the one whose transgression is forgiven, whose sin is covered. Blessed is the man against whom the Lord counts no iniquity, and in whose spirit there is no deceit... I acknowledged my sin to you, and I did not cover my iniquity; I said, "I will confess my transgressions to the Lord," and you forgave the iniquity of my sin.

   3.1. ***"Blessed is the man against whom the Lord counts no iniquity, and in whose spirit there is no deceit..."***

      3.1.1. Notice, the Lord does not COUNT the INIQUITY because DECEIT, which is the INIQUITY, has been removed from that person.

   3.2. ***"I acknowledged my sin to you, and I did not cover my iniquity..."***

      3.2.1. Note, it was because the the INIQUITY was not covered up or kept hidden.

      3.2.2. Moreover, because the INIQUITY was not HIDDEN, the TRANSGRESSION was easily CONFESSED.

      3.2.3. In other words, we cannot make a TRUTHFUL confession until we ACKNOWLEDGE the iniquity that triggers the act of our TRANSGRESSIONS.

4. Ezekiel 37:23 (ESV): They shall not defile them-selves anymore with their idols and their detestable things, or with any of their trans-gressions. But I will save them from all the backsliding in which they have sinned, and will cleanse them; and they shall be my people, and I will be their God.

   4.1. ***"But I will save them from all the back-sliding in which they have sinned, and will cleanse them..."***

       4.1.1. Notice again, God CLEANSES the INIQUITY to save us from the BACKSLIDING.

   4.2. ***"They shall not defile themselves anymore with their idols and their detestable things, or with any of their transgressions."***

       4.2.1. In other words, Just like IDOLS that were made according to the imagination of a person, we will no longer defile our-selves with the things we create out of our imaginations.

Lastly, consider how Ezekiel 37 tells us that the Lord will save from the "*backsliding*." Backsliding... also known as *regression*.

Regression, according to psychology, is an unconscious, emotional defense mechanism where an individual's personality reverts to an ear-lier point of development and portray behaviors similar to behaviors of that earlier point when felt confronted with threatening or objectionable situations.[41]

Therefore, if backsliding is the biblical expression for regression, then let us put Ezekiel 37 into context. "They shall not defile themselves anymore with their idols and their detestable things, or with any of their transgressions. But I will save them from all [their *regression*] in which they have sinned and will cleanse them; and they shall be my people, and I will be their God.

Jesus Christ for a moment was struck with hook-threaded whips across his back *for our backsliding*. Christ was intentional about being whipped across His back those many lashes, so we would be afforded freedom from our backsliding.

Some of us may have been able to put our actions to pause. But all of us are guilty of backsliding. We backslide into ways of thinking. We backslide into attitudes. We backslide into mannerisms. We have even *backslidden* into emotiveness that is not becoming of our freedom found in Jesus Christ.

Going From Well to Going through "Hell."

---

[41] Smith, Tracy http://www.e-counseling.com/mental-health/understanding-regression-psychology/ November 9, 2018.

Looking back, I realize that my life had been riddled with radical dispensations of backsliding. Still, in all of this time, I had not considered that these radical dispensations were the equivalent to a cancer patient coming out of remission. We are remiss to assume there are no experienced times of great malady after treatment.

I had never considered the idea that the ailment of my condition was the actual cure to my pain. Up until this moment, I never considered what does a life pursuant to discipleship in Christ looks like when that life is asked to "pick up it's cross?" In the spirit of transparency... the cross is scary!

Make not mistake, fear is the first sign of sin but fear is not sin. Furthermore, the assertion that "FEAR IS NOT" of God, is a contradiction of Proverbs 15.24 which tells us, "The prudent sees danger and hides himself, but the simple go on and suffer for it." When Christ was tempted by Satan to cast himself of the roof of the temple, Christ's replay was, "Test not, the Lord your God." In other words, the fear of the Lord provides you wisdom to know that there are are some things we should be alarmed of. There are some things we should have a healthy fear of.

We should *fear* enslavement to sin. We should *fear* entanglement to bad company, for it corrupts good morals. We should *fear* failing to obtain grace of God. We should *fear* heresy. We should *fear* becoming intolerant of sound doctrine. We should *fear* not being counted in that number on that great and dreadful day of our Lord's return. We should *fear* the one who can, not only take physical life from us but also the the after-life, as well. Lastly, we should *fear* the loss of a sound mind. In contrast, it is the *spirit of fear* that God did not give. The spirit of fear produces anxiety, desperation, and self-preservation, just to name but a few.

Holy Spirit, also known as the Spirit of the Lord, is a Spirit of power, love, and soundness of mind. Power, love, and soundness of mind are characteristic of Holy Spirit. So, when I say fear is the first sign of sin. I am not saying that fear is a sign of sinfulness. When I say fear is the first sign of sin, I am saying that the byproduct of sinfulness is behavior registered, stemming, and triggered by fear. When we are in sin, we act in accordance with the *spirit of fear.* The first telltale sign of sin is a *spirit of fear.* We can see this clearly in Genesis 3.

Adam and Eve sought to cover their nakedness and hide their sinful transgression by making clothes with fig leaves for their nakedness. Their iniquity propelled them into transgression, as they went into hiding attempting to cover their sins.

God responds by dealing with their iniquity, the hidden sin, first by asking them, "where are you?" God, then, deals with their sinful behavior, the transgression, by providing them with new coverings. Killing what He loved, washing them with the lamb's blood, and then covering them with the lamb's skin to cover their nakedness and transgression. God finally deals with their iniquity. By quarantining them from eternity and placing them into time, He provides them a medium for remission of sin. God declares redemption for their souls and gives them time for repentance.

Furthermore, God clears them away from the temptation. His refusal to allow them access to the tree of life was not a consequence but a concession. God did not want humanity to be stuck in eternity as sinners. Thus, He sets them into time to cure their sickness of sin.

Again, the nature of our flesh in its battle against the Spirit is to seek the least threatening way of trying to satisfy our ongoing for God while looking for the loopholes. In contrast, it is the nature of Holy Spirit to point to the faulty area(s) in us that need to be addressed. This is what is being explained in Ephesians 4.22–24 when Paul says, "put off your old self, which belongs to your former manner of life and is corrupt through deceitful desires, and to be renewed in the "*spirit*" of your minds..."[42] take note that word "*spirit*" keeps popping up. Scripture, here, references the renewing of the "*spirit*" of our minds. Similar to the "spirit of the prophets", that is subject to the prophets, our minds are subject to the "*spirit*" of our mind. This "*spirit*" of the mind is also what can be best described as the life-giving essence of our thought life.

Looking back at the dichotomy of our humanity found in Romans 7, the battle between the *Spirit* and the flesh can be summarized as the battle between two minds. The first mind being "the mind in the Flesh, the second being "mind of the *Spirit*." Our "*spirit*" mind needs to be aligned with the mind of Holy Spirit.

If you will recall, we are made in the image and likeness of God. We are in similar manner to the Trinity. As God is Father, Son, and Holy Spirit, we are Spirit, soul, and body. When we become born again, the Holy Spirit's work occurs in the three spheres of our spirit, our souls, and the behaviors of our body. When we become born again, the Holy Spirit transposes our spirit with His own Spirit, our souls then become interconnected with the soul of Spirit, and our bodies respond in suit by acting in accordance to the Spirits' prompting

---

[42] Holy Bible, Ephesians 4.22-24.

of our behavior. To bring greater clarity to Holy Spirit's work within us, J.I. Packer explains this:

"God is triune; there are with the Godhead three persons, the Father, the Son, the Holy Spirit; and the work of salvation is one in which all three act together, the Father purposing redemption, the Son securing it, and the Holy Spirit applying it."[43]

Remember what was previously stated, our sinfulness exists on three spheres: inherently, in our nature, and through our will. The old self refuses to go away. Thus, when we become born again, we are trading the old nature for a new nature. However, part of trading in the old nature for the new nature is a deliberate act of putting off your old self and putting on the new self. This is the new-life renewal continuum of our sanctification process.

Science inadvertently speaks of this truth. The Pauli exclusion principle states, "two substances cannot occupy the same space simultaneously."[44]

---

[43]   Packer, J.I. Knowing God. Illinois: InterVarsity, 1973, p. 20.

[44]   http://en.wikipedia.org/wiki/Pauli_exclusion_principle

The Spirit wants what is contrary to what the flesh wants. And the flesh, contrary to the Spirit. As a result, a conflict arises in our being. For some of us, this creates times of crisis within us. But as John Maxwell defines it, "times of crisis are an intense time of difficulty requiring a decision that will be a turning point."[45]

My life was at a moment of crisis. There I was – jobless, directionless, and purposeless, so I thought. I did not realize it then but my journey was at a turning point towards my ultimate destination for conformity to the likeness of Christ.

However, before the turning point in my life would be actualized, it was imperative for me to come under the light of Holy Spirit and surrender to the scrutiny of correction. I would have to allow the Holy Spirit to point to areas in my life that were still submitted to the flesh. Thus, I needed to humbly receive Holy Spirit's view of these areas in my life as the correct view of them.

First, I had to recognize that my layoff was not the filthy knife being twisted slowing into my gut, as I had internalized it to be. On the contrary, my layoff served as the sterile scalpel God used to remove the cancerous tumor within me. There was a history of trauma I had experience, even

---

[45]   Maxwell, John Leading Through Crisis, p. 2.

before my experience with the elder, I had tucked away deep within me. Holy Spirit was bringing me back to the root of my embedded afflictions.

God was causing me to revisit the day my innocence was robbed and a time where knowingness was awakened before its time. God had taken me back to my exposure to pornography and alcohol at the tender early age of eight years old. It was at the age of eight when I took my first sip of the inebriating elixir and fixed my gaze upon the seductress of adult films.

It occurred during a time when I was forced apart from my mother and sister because of inconvenient circumstances. My father's addictions forced my mother to make choices she should not have had to make. Thus, instead of causing my sister and I to experience the shelter system or placement in foster care, she opted to have my sister stay with a family friend and for me to remain with my grandmother.

Living apart from my mother had been convoluted experience. Although I had a place to stay, I frequently found myself staying in various other family member's homes from time to time. This type of uncertainty and instability left me having to fend for myself more often than not. This type of living structure made me susceptible to a number of different safety and risk issues. Mine happened to be pornography and alcohol.

For years, I had tucked this exposure away under the category of cultural norms. My Hispanic heritage rendered a false claim of patriarchal and misogynistic undertones. For the men in my family, exposure to alcohol and illicit sexual material was seen as an eventuality. This eventuality was viewed in a perverted sort of "rites-of-passage" that ushered a young boy into manhood. This twisted notion of male maturity was even accompanied by celebratory nuances of a young man awakening into full adult male-hood.

No one had ever told me that this was a form of sexual abuse. Nor did anyone ever sit me down and help me process what my under-developed adolescent mind was unable to understand. Instead, these two substances would become the agents subsidizing my outlook on pleasure. Ironically, these same two substances would also become the agents and resources for my pain management. And manage my pain they did because they never provided any true pain relief.

Fast-forwarding towards the present, Holy Spirit began to show me that our minds take in these outward pressures, associates them with past pain, and immediately becomes consumed, swilled down, swallowed up, and even suffocated by the compression of suffering. It is the natural order of the mind to take in, absorb, and swallow that which is placed upon us, while simultaneously associating these pressures with feelings of past events we have encountered. The duress I found myself experiencing introduced intense levels of pressure which placed me in **the quicksand**.

Whatever Happen to Deliverance?

I'm sure you are asking exactly what I had asked continually through this point of my life. Whatever happened to deliverance? What happened to the transforming work of Holy Spirit at the point of conversion? For many of us, deliverance holds the idea of demonic forces occupying our bodies requiring an exorcism. Now, this in not to say that deliverance, in the manner to which I am describing, is not a reality. However, it is not the usual, it is the occasional. Our usual forms of deliverances are happening in the subtle changes of conversions, shifts in our perspectives, and our transformations from conformity to the patterns of this world to conformity to the likeness of Christ.

Deliverance, I discovered, is the power Holy Spirit equips us with to act in accordance to the changes in behaviors that are required. We are not immune to the evil doings of "Self" unconditionally.

However, through the new nature ascribed to us by Holy Spirit's indwelling, we become conditioned to resist the temptations of "Self."

Romans 6.12–14 says it this way...

> ***"Therefore, do not let sin reign in your mortal body, so that you obey its desires. And do not offer any parts of it to sin as weapons for unrighteousness. But as those who are alive from the dead, offer yourselves to God, and all the parts of yourselves to God as weapons for righteousness. For sin will not rule over you, because you are not under the law but under grace."***[46]

Do you know what God and sin have in common? They both require our willingness. Our volition is necessary. It is through our faculties of will that we make a choice to offer or not offer ourselves to God or to sin. Thus, deliverance is two-fold. First, Christ canceled our debt, which disarmed Satan and his angels, the rulers and authorities, as is in accordance to Colossians 2.13.[47] Second, because sin's rule over us is dismantled,

---

[46] Holy Bible, Romans 6.12-14.

[47] Ibid., Colossians 2.13.

sin no longer tells us what to do. We can now tell sin what to do with itself.

Deliverance in the Hebrew is defined as the *"rescuing."* God not only removes the powers of the dark forces upon our lives, He also releases the "spirit" of our minds to become renewed in our thoughts, our feelings, and our behaviors. Consequently, we are rescued from faulty thinking, feeling, and behaving.

Philippians 4.13 tells us, "Therefore, my dear friends, just as you have always obeyed, so now, not only in my presence but even more in my absence, *work out your own salvation* with fear and in trembling. For it is God who is working in you *both to will and work* according to his good purpose." And in this regard, we are delivered and being delivered.

Yet, there is an inadvertent yearning to experience the ecstatic and mystical. We want the immediate dramatization of the transformative without the labor of discipline that comes with being transformed. What continues then is the ongoing pull of the flesh that I like to refer to as *"Sin-ertia".*

Chapter 6

SIN-ERTIA

· ·

I nertia is the resistance of any object to any change in its motion. This includes changes to the object's speed, or direction of motion. However, inertia is not simply inactivity or inaction. An aspect of inertia is the tendency of an object to keep moving in a singular direction at a constant pace when there isn't a force to counter its motion.[48] Thus, that object cannot and will not change its course unless confronted by an opposing force.

Now, if we were to apply this concept to our Christian journey, we would quickly realize it is our likelihood to continue to act in pace with the flesh unless the momentum of the flesh is met by the impact of Holy Spirit. Life before Christ has an established momentum in its carnal nature. And

---

[48] "Inertia." <u>The American Heritage Collage Dictionary.</u> 4th ed. 2002.

because of this established momentum of carnality, we are prone to keeping within the trajectory of life's course when there isn't any alternate force to act upon it. I call this, *"Sin-ertia"*

> *"It starts out normally, with the joyfulness of liberation... Before long, the natural joy will undergo a malignant change; it will be replaced by pride... in a day or a week or a few months, with a reoccurrence of an impulse... It comes subtly and innocuously, certainly not as a conscious desire... sometimes the desire appears unconscious... the downfall can seem for all the world like a demonically mystical happening... the habit is now an integral part of life... the desire to do the behavior surfaces like a reflex..."*[49]

We are truly creatures of habit prone to habituation from a mind calibrated by patterns. If what causes me pain is relieved by acts of pleasure, then behaving for pleasure keeps me from pain. Remember, the nature of our flesh in its battle against the Spirit naturally seeks the least threatening way of trying to satisfy our ongoing for God,

---

[49] May, Gerald, p. 48, 49.

while we still look for loopholes. In short, we love serving God on our own terms.

We are told in the book of 1 Kings that king Ahab was one of the most notorious kings of the Northern Kingdom of Israel. 1 Kings 16.30 tells us, he was "more evil than all who were before him." The next verse adds, "if following the sins of Jeroboam were not enough, he also marries Jezebel, daughter of Ethbaal, king of the Sidonians."[50]

Let's make some things clear. Ahab was evil. Scripture tells us he followed the sins of king Jeroboam. Now, this fact is important to understand because Jeroboam was the first king of Northern Israel. And as his claiming act of fame, Jeroboam influenced Israel towards idol worship by strategically erecting two golden calves within their main temples of worship.

Ahab held to this practice and enthusiastically misguided the Northern kingdom towards idolatry. Still, Ahab was not satisfied with this level of wickedness. He needed to be more wicked than any king before him. Ergo, he pursued greater depths of wickedness by strategically deciding to marry Jezebel, daughter of Ethbaal, king of the

---

[50]   Holy Bible, 1 Kings 16.30.

Sidonians. Make no mistake, Ahab was perfectly aware of who he would be getting involved with.

This marriage was a marriage of moral reprehensibility. To grasp the depths this unholy union, we will need to explore the downward distance of Ahab's sinfulness and to grasp the pull of "*Sinertina*." Let us take a sneak peek into the roots of this "*cult*" of personality.

As previously stated, Ahab betroths and weds the insidious princess of the Sidonians. Her father, King Ethbaal, was an avid worshiper of Baal. His name, Ethbaal, means, one under Baal's ownership or possession. Ethbaal being a mere worshiper of Baal is an understatement. To put this plainly, Ethbaal was a vessel for the spirit of Baal and a proxy for Baal's presence. In similar manner, Jezebel retained submission to the dark principality. Her name speaks for itself, princess of Baal. More accurately, Jezebel means she who is in allegiance and pledged to Baal.[51]

1 Kings 21.25 tells us Ahab "*devoted*" himself to doing what was evil. Ahab was a malicious anti-christ type who hid in plain view. Jezebel was nothing more than his favorite assassin. If Ahab was the head of the cartel, Jezebel would be his go-to *sacario*. Let us not be mistaken, Jezebel was

---

[51] Strongs, James. The Exhaustive Concordance of the Bible. Abington Press, 6th ed. 1890.

dreadful but she only as dreadful as the husband she was married to.

Further into 1 Kings 21, you will find a historical account of a man by the name of Naboth. Naboth was the owner of a small vineyard adjacent to Ahab's palace. In a spirit of covetousness, Ahab attempts to purchase this piece of land. However, this land was a family inheritance.[52] Thus, Naboth refused to place it up for sale. We are then told that Ahab returns home despondent, refusing to eat, and laying on his bed in a pout while he waited for his wife's returned.

Seeing her husband at a low, Jezebel proceeds to asks her husband why he seemed so disheartened. He proceeds to explain to his "concerned" wife how he attempted to offer a "good" price for the purchase of piece of land. Yet, the owner refused to take his offer. According to Ahab, Naboth was acting "unreasonably." In response, Jezebel attends to her husband with a little pampering. After coddling her man-child of a husband, she then proceeds to plot a conspiracy against Naboth. Her plot was successful.

On the surface, we witness a crafty Jezebel succeed in the assassination of Naboth. But, within the underbelly of this ploy, we find an even craftier

---

[52] Holy Bible, 1 Kings 21.1.

Ahab who works his wife to do his dirty work. Yet, even this is not what made Ahab more wicked than Jezebel.

What made Ahab was worse than Jezebel was that he knew *God.*

Scripture tells us, "For it would have been better for them not to have known the way of righteousness than, after knowing it, to turn back from the holy command delivered to them."[53] In 1 Kings chapter 21.19, we read the word of the Lord spoken by Elijah. He declared disaster on the house of Ahab as a result of this heinous act against Naboth. Yet, in verse twenty-seven we read, "When Ahab heard these words, he tore his clothes, he put on sack cloth over his body, and fasted." Verse twenty-nine then follows with, "because Ahab humbled himself before me..."[54] God relented from striking Ahab. Again, Ahab *knew* God.

Ahab was well-versed in the Torah and the promises held within the reestablished covenant of Deuteronomy. Ahab knew very well that at the very heart of God's character is compassion. If you

---

[53] Ibid., 2 Peter 2.21.

[54] Ibid., 1 Kings 21.27-29.

will compare the similarities between Ahab's cries of mercy before God to how Ahab was able to gain sympathy from his wife on their marriage bed, we would be remiss to overlook this one essential characteristic about Ahab. Ahab was awfully good and craftily skilled at "*knowing*" who he was dealing with and how to deal with them. However, God also *knows* who he deals with and is able to see the intentions of the heart, as well as judge the thoughts of humanity.[55]

Later, in 1 Kings 22.22, we read of a spirit amongst the armies of the heavenly hosts who came forward and told God that he would go and entice Ahab. God then asks this spirit how he would do so. The spirit replies, "I will *become* a lying spirit in the mouths of all his prophets." To be clear, God did not cause a lie. God does not the lie nor does God tempt Ahab in a lie. James 1.14 says it best. "Each person is tempted when they are drawn away and enticed by their own evil desires."[56]

Ahab had made a habit of living according to his deceptions, his con-artistry, his manipulations, and his spiritual justifications. Ahab had "*devoted*" himself to doing what was evil in the Lord's eyes.

---

[55] Ibid., Hebrews 4.12.

[56] Ibid., James 1.14.

All that Ahab had previously sown in his sinfulness was now prepared to be reaped. Furthermore, Ahab made it customary to live according to false prophesies. He recruited false prophets of Yahweh who would prophesy for his benefit as opposed to the truth.

We are just as guilty of recruiting false prophets when we are seeking the answers we desire as opposed to the answers God seeks to give. Let us never forget that we begin store up wrath for ourselves when we become self-purposed, self-seeking, and selfishly intended when we do not obey the truth in accordance to God.[57]

Ahab had a myriad of evils he devoutly committed himself to. Ahab consistently resisted changing his actions. His tendency to keep moving in constant pace with his sinfulness could no longer be turned. *Sin-ertia* had already been set in motion, at such a great momentum, that even repentance no longer proved empowering for change.

Although it is the most powerful tool in the transforming life of a Christian, Repentance can become powerless. Thus, we should never be self-deceived into thinking that we can return to the outward performances of repentance like a

---

[57] Ibid,. Romans 2.8.

bulimic who spews out what was just ingested. Like spiritual bulimics, many of us are guilty of vomiting up the fruits of repentance. We love to binge on self-indulgence.

After we have overtly indulged, we begin to feel guilty. As a result, we seek to relieve ourselves from the shame of our guilty pleasure through a process of catharsis. The catharsis or purging, if you will, succeeds in only starving our flesh. And like a bulimic who assumes that because starvation keeps them from gaining weight, we too, assume that because the consequences of sin has not reared its ugly head, we have averted punishment.

Barclay tells us...

> *"So long as a man in his heart of hearts hates sin and hates himself for sinning, so long as he knows that he is sinning, he is never beyond repentance, and, therefore, never beyond forgiveness; but once a man begins to revel in sin, and to make sin the deliberate policy of his life, and loses all sense of the terror and the awfulness of sin and also the feeling of self-disgust, he is on the way to death, for he is on the way*

*to a state where the idea of repentance
will not, and cannot, enter his head."[58]*

The author of Hebrews tells us:

*"And make sure that there isn't any
immoral or irreverent person like Esau,
who sold his birthright in exchange for
one meal. For you know that later, when
he wanted to inherit the blessing, he was
rejected because he didn't find any oppor-
tunity for repentance, though he sought it
with tears."[59]*

**Repentance becomes powerless when
it finds no further opportunities for
repentance.**

Realize, we can *"fall short"* of the Grace of God.
This is why it is so important for us to have a cor-
rect and proper understand of the application of
Grace. Grace is not liberty as much as it is *freedom.*

---

[58] Baryclay, William. *The Gospel of Matthew.* 2 vols. The
Daily Study Bible series. 2nd ed. Edinburgh: Saint
Andrews Press. 1964.

[59] Holy Bible, Hebrews 12.15-18.

In Grace we find liberty, but in *freedom* we do not find sin.

Sin's Spin Cycle

I, too, was caught in sin's spin cycle. And because it started to gain momentum, I now required an interjecting agent to challenge the trajectory of sin upon my life by providing a counter force that would shift my direction. This unstoppable force of sin had to be met by the immovable impact of Holy Spirit for me to come to a complete *halt*.

My terrible loss of position was actually a triumphant shifting of the tide. What appeared as a forceful change in my life was the spiritual changing in trajectory and the shifting towards a correct direction. What Holy Spirit had orchestrated in the immediate change of environment, immediate change of culture, immediate change of pace, was the urgency of God to change my direction and move me towards His correct path.

> *When I thought I had met the fork in the road, God showed Himself to be a way maker and set a course for me to go straight.*

Chapter 7

THE RIGHT SIDE
OF THE ROAD

. . . .

Some time had passed until I found myself, once again, in a ministerial capacity. In my newly found position as a staff pastor of a pretty lucrative ministry, I assumed my previous ministerial predicaments had seen their last days. This was not the case. So, when I took notice of similar occurrences to those from my previous ministry experience, I also took notice of the fact that my mind would shift towards those previous feelings and thoughts, as well. It is the nature of the mind to assess our experiences based upon previous experiences that we have determined to either be pleasurable or painful. Thus, how we assess a situation will depend on how we have defined a previously similar situation.

1 Samuel 18.10–11 tells us, "The next day an evil spirit sent from God took control of Saul, and he began to rave inside the palace. David was playing the lyre as usual, but Saul was holding a spear, and he threw it, thinking, "I'll pin David to the wall." But David got away from him twice."[60]

Saul was the anointed king of Israel. However, Saul was also out of control. So much so, that while worship was being conducted, Saul would go into fits of rage. Saul would occasionally pick up his favorite spear and chuck it at David. What is remarkable about this story is David's reaction. David never picks up the thrown spear and throws it back. He never seeks to retaliate. Instead, David learns to dodge spears. We know this to be true because the Scripture clearly tells us this wasn't David's first time: *"But David got away from him twice."*

On this next path of my journey, God was doing something new with me. Here, Holy Spirit reminded me of the words found in Isaiah 43.18–19, "Remember not the former things, nor consider the things of old. Behold, I am doing a new thing..." The word of God tells us here, *"remember not, nor consider."* When God affords us a new beginning, He admonishes us to stop considering the events

---

[60] Ibid., 1 Samuel 18. 10–11.

of the past. This is easier said than done. It is the events of the past that mold and shape our perceptions of present events. What we learn from our past events help us to forge into the future. But memories of the past can also keep us from new experiences based upon what appears to be perceivable harm at present.

The Lord will allow us to experience similar scenarios for two reasons. One, God is our redeemer who seeks to provide us with opportunities to redeem our past. Two, God is our restorer who seeks to repair us. Much of the pain we have endured in our past can continue to traumatize us into our future unless the memories of those past events experience renovation, repair, restoration. At this point of my life, I had to accept the scalpel that God had chosen to cut out the "tumor."

God uses the worse of them to shape the best of us, by allowing the best of us to be impacted by the worse of them in such a way that, even the reflection of the worse of them propels the best of us to seek better in Him.

Chapter 8

STAY IN YOUR LANE

. . . .

Holy Spirit is in the very order of Holy God and the Holy Son. There is a divine arrangement within the Trinity that neither of the three dare break. Each speaks of one another, and none acts contrary to the other. The three *are* one, and yet, the three *are* individually their own. A primary example of this can be found in John 15.26 which states, "But when the Helper comes, whom I will send to you from the Father, the Spirit of truth, who proceeds from the Father, he will bear witness about me."[61]

George P. Pardington stated it this way:

> *In general, the working of each member of the Trinity is this: in every divine activity, the power to arrange proceeds from the*

---

[61] Ibid., John 15.26.

Son; and the power to perfect proceeds from the Spirit. Consequently, the official work of the Holy Spirit in every phase and sphere of the divine activity is to bring forward to completion that which has been conceived by the Father and executed by the Son.[62]

Notice how Holy Spirit, the Helper, the Spirit of Truth, is from the Father. Yet, Holy Spirit bears witness to Jesus. These three personalities are simpatico, full of likeness, like mindedness, and complete agreement. This sympathetic relationship is a unique bond in complete harmony with itself and still manages to maintain distinction between the three individual personalities. But there is another relationship that is of similar characteristic to this relationship but is not in the likeness of its holiness. As Holy Spirit testifies to His Spirit, so too, carnality draws to carnality. This relationship is what I like to call a "*sin-patico*" relationship.

---

[62] Pardington, George P. Outline Studies in Christian Doctrine, Pennsylvania: Christian Publications, p. 301.

SIN-PATICO

"*Sin-patico*" Christian personalities can be easily identified by their innate propensity to seek gaps and ambiguous inconsistencies in Scriptural text. "*Sin-patico*" Christian personalities can also be identified by their tendency to align themselves to dogmas and argue over the relevance of biblical doctrines. "*Sin-patico*" Christian personalities love the appears of peacemakers whose philosophy is that can *agree to disagree*. Yet, we find this idea nowhere in Scripture. Instead, we are admonished, "Can two walk together unless they agree?"[63] In short, carnal Christianity only begets carnal Christian relationships. Thus, you find some Christian relationship as being "*Sin-patico*." Let us take this moment to reflect on these several passages:

"If you do what is right, won't you be accepted? But if you do not do what is right, sin is crouching at the door. It's desire is for you, but you must rule over it."

- Genesis 4.7

---

[63] Holy Bible, Amos 3.3.

"For though they knew God, they did not glorify Him as God or show gratitude. Instead, their thinking became worthless, and their senseless hearts were darkened... Therefore, God delivers them over in the desire of their hearts..."

- Romans 1.21- 23

"Do not be deceived: "Bad company ruins good morals." Wake up from your drunken stupor, as is right, and do not go on sinning."

- I Corinthians 15.33

"For the time will come when people will not tolerate sound doctrine, but according to their own desires, will multiply teachers for themselves because they have an itch to hear what they want to hear.

2 Timothy 4.3

Christians who will qualify your incorrectness are not your brothers or sisters. If they hide the truth for you, they will keep the truth from you.

When Jesus first sends out His disciples, He tells them to go and proclaim good news. However, He further tells His disciples that they will be flogged, dragged to court, delivered over to death, and will be hated. In short, Jesus was sending them into *hostile* territory. The irony of this is that Jesus was sending them to the community of alleged believers. He was sending them to the people of Israel.

Jesus then tells His disciples, "Don't assume that I came to bring peace on the earth. I did not come to bring peace, but a sword."[64] This is the same Jesus who in His sermon on the mount tells us, "Blessed are the peace makers, they will be called children of God." Contradictory? Absolutely not. There is huge difference between peace *keeping* and peace *making*.

In 1 Chronicles 17, we are told that king David was visited by the prophet Nathan who proceeds to prophesy and tell David what God's intentions were for Him. After David was told how God would make his name as great as the great names of the earth; how God would build him a house for him and his household; how God would guarantee that one of his sons would always occupy his throne; and how God was going to secure peace all Israel,

---

[64]   Ibid., Matthew 10.34.

king David then follows this prophetic declaration over his life by organizing a military campaign to actualize Israel's position as a formidable nation.

David furthers his efforts by placing garrisons at strategic regions that surrounded Israel. As a final result, David secured a peaceful environment for all of Israel. All of these great exploits can be read in Scripture. Do you know what we don't read in Scripture? David signed peace treaties.

God promised peace would be secured as a result of David's diligence to *make* peace for Israel. David's military campaigns not only high-lighted strategies to conquer his enemies. They also included plans to establish garrisons at spe-cific locations to secure peace within and without Israel's proximity.

These garrisons that David erected were nothing more than regional barracks that pos-sessed the established authority of his kingdom. These garrisons can be likened to military com-pounds where troops are deployed for the sole purpose of policing the area and protecting against enemy hostiles. These compounds are populated with military combatants trained to engage unrest. However, their training does not include redirecting antagonistic behavior through "positive reinforcement." The mission for these combatants was a simple one. Bring about compliance to the kingdom.

This insight provides a clear understanding of what Paul wrote in 2 Corinthians 10:3–6.[65]

> *"For though we live in the body, we do not wage war in an unspiritual way, since the weapons of our warfare are not worldly, but are powerful through God for the demolition of strongholds. We demolish arguments and every high-minded thing that is raised up against the knowledge of God, taking every thought captive to obey Christ. And we are ready to punish any disobedience, once your obedience has been confirmed."*

The weapons of our warfare are powerful through God. Our weapons are spiritual and not of the flesh. Our weapons are for demolishing strongholds of ideas, elevated feelings, emotional attachments, fallacies, pretentiousness, habitual patterns of thinking, and the like. But more important than this, these weapons of ours are not only for our defense. They are designed for the offensive.

---

[65] Ibid., 2 Corinthians 10.3–6.

We miss the mark when we remain in a defensive stance. Christ tells us that upon the rock of His truth, the gates of hell will not prevail. The power of the weapon of Christ's truth is most effective *at the gates of hell*. The gate of hell is the one place Christ guarantees us that the weapon of *Truth* will not fail. A defensive stance means we are trying to *keep* something we have from being taken. Whereas the offensive stance means we are trying to *take* something we don't have into our possession.

The *peace makers* are blessed because they are on the offensive seeking to *take* what is not yet in their possession. But they do not stop there. They also *make* peace by establishing a defensive wall. Peacemaking, therefore, is twofold. First, there is the offensive stance for the *taking* over the hostile area. Second, there is the defensive stance for the *making* of the hostile area into an area of peace. We are guilty of engaging in our warfare backward.

We exhaust much of our energy trying to *keep* the enemy away or pushing him back. Instead, we must *take* the hostile areas the enemy has occupied in our lives, then *make* that hostile area an environment of peace. We are easily deceived by the enemy into thinking that we have to take a defensive stance, we have to stand guard, and keep watch. Keeping only to a defense posture never helps us to press forward and gain ground. One thing about Satan, he is perfectly okay with our local wins just as long as it distracts us from our global victories.

Furthermore, we will exasperate ourselves if we fail to *make* a stronghold for ourselves through Christ. Again, the weapons of our warfare demolish arguments, every high-minded thing, and all that is raised up against our conformity to God. Yet, Paul tells us that we are to *take* every thought *captive* to the obedience of Christ.

Let's take a logical look at this for a moment. Do you think that things like dignity, purity, and integrity are found in Satan? Then how are we declaring to take dignity, purity, and integrity back from him? In Satan's possession, dignity, purity, and integrity are perverted and false identifications of their truthful selves. Thus, we are to *take* possession of the hostile environment of worthlessness and establish dignity found in Christ, we are to *take* the places of immodesty and *make* purity realized by the washing of Holy Spirit, and we are to *take* the areas of villainy and *make* integrity stand in accordance to Christ's truth. Hence, when Paul says "and we are ready to punish any disobedience, once your obedience has been confirmed", he is essentially saying that we are intended on *making* the hostile environments of our lives places of peace by authority of Christ, our Prince of Peace.

Robert Frost said, "Good fences make good neighbors." Twice, Proverbs makes a similar statement. "Don't move an ancient boundary marker..."[66] Both these statements point to an all-important truth. We must know our boundaries.

Boundaries, I have learned, are not so much for others as much as for ourselves. Boundaries, like good fences, are land markers that we can see through. A boundary, like a good fence, gives us the ability to keep our space without isolating ourselves from the rest of the world. Christ, His word of truth, and Holy Spirt, the Spirit of truth, provide great boundaries. Let us never forget that, "Everything is permissible, but not all beneficial."[67]

---

[66] Ibid., Proverbs 22.28, 23.10.

[67] Ibid., 1 Corinthians 6.12.

Chapter 9

STOP WALKING AND JUST STAND

. . . .

The word *"experience"* is so ambiguous and comprising of all that it becomes rather useless.[68] This is especially true of our Christian experience.

Paramount to the Christian walk is transformation. Transformation, however, is not merely an *"experience,"* it is a work. Transformation requires more than just experiencing the transforming work taking effect. Transformation requires our participation in order for it to become grafted into our new nature. The Holy Spirit's work within us is the same yet distinct to each of us. How Holy Spirit work's in you may not be the exact work in me. Yet, God is the same, yesterday, today, and

---

[68]   Whitehead, James D., Evelyn Easton, Method in Ministry, Minnesota: Winston Press, 1980, P. 53.

forever. We, however, are not always the same and do require individual detailing.

Our Christian experiences are shaped through a correlation of revelation, personal realizations, traditions of truth as we see it, and cultural influences that begin to pass through the filtration system of Scripture to help us establish what we call our convictions. Therefore, the term *"experience"* fails to explain the potency, diversity, and exclusivity needed to define the fullness of the Christian journey.

My life, until now, had been nothing more than a series of experience seeking. The experiences I was seeking were the experiences of others and none of my own. I was chasing the next person's journey. By doing so, I was neglecting my own. I viewed my own experiences with God as failed experiences compared to the illustrious testimonials parading the pulpits. I reasoned that unless my testimony sounded like and looked like theirs, I have not had a true experience with God.

My mistake was leaning on the idea that I should be experiencing the same experiences as the rest of my counterparts. Yet, all God desired for me was to uniquely experience Him for myself. Speaking to Moses, God said, "I am Yahweh. I appeared to Abraham, Isaac, and Jacob as God

Almighty, but I did not reveal My name Yahweh to them."[69]

God uses two names to describe Himself here. He begins by explaining to Moses that He is and was known by his forefathers as *El Shaddai*; The all-powerful, all sufficient one, God Almighty. However, El Shaddai, the all-powerful, all sufficient one, and God Almighty are more of descriptions of His character, as opposed to who He is. Nevertheless, God does not end their conversation here.

God proceeds to tell Moses that His name is *Yahweh*; Jehovah, *your* Lord. It wasn't enough for God to have Moses know him according to what He does. God was not satisfied with Moses only knowing Him by what qualities He possessed. God would not accept Moses simply knowing Him as the God of His forefathers, Abraham, Isaac, and Jacob. On the contrary, it was God's deepest desire for Moses to know Him in a personal, explicit, and exclusive way. God desired to be the God of Moses.

God is not satisfied with us knowing him by reputation. His hope and desire is for us to know Him in an intimate and personal

---

[69] Holy Bible, Exodus 6.2–3.

way. So, God reintroduces Himself as "I am Jehovah, your God!"

In this same way, God was longing for me to know Him as "*My God; the God of Ray.*" And "*the God of Ray*" needed to be an exclusive and personal God to me. His desire was for me to have Him finally for myself. His desire is for us to have Him for ourselves. His desires is to honorably mention us in that great list of names as Abraham, Isaac, and Jacob, as well. What He does not want is for us to chase after the God of the others. Never once had I considered that God did not want to be the God of others. He desired to be "*My God.*" He desires to be "*Your God.*"

The God of Others

When our predicament meets our purpose, there we will find God looking to see if we will agree to align ourselves with His way. When our predicament meets with our purpose, God is intended on changing our heart, mind, soul, and strength. Failure to embrace this change will always result in remaining in the predicament and our spiritual growth remaining stunted. However, when we come to agreement with the aligned purposes of God, we succeed in initiating spiritual growth.

God changes the "*Nature*" of who we are because we are inherently sinful. Yet, He does not change the "*who we are*" because who we are culturally, ethnically, in personality, and in physicality are all sacred to God. Thus, the way in which we comply with God through our predicaments will impact the nature by which we perceive how Holy Spirit is leading us.

Reflection can be limited to our cultural traditions and personal traditions of truth we have been accustomed to. The sacred nature of who we are culturally, ethnically, in personality, and in physicality are just as sacred to God as they are to us. Consequently, what we are culturally, ethnically, in personality, and in physicality do not define how our purpose in Christ is to be defined.

At our rebirth, Christ now sets the definition of who we are within the constructs of our cultures, ethnicities, our personalities, and physicality. In Exodus 19.5, God invites Israel to be His own personal possession amongst other people groups. The King James Version of the Bible properly describes this invitation as becoming a "*peculiar people*" amongst all people.

1 Peter 4:4 describes our "*peculiarities*" in relation to this world as a surprise to them because you and I no longer plunge ourselves into the same flow of living. The apostle further adds that we will

be slandered, insulted, made fun of because of our new and *"peculiar"* nature. But, being called to this *"peculiarity"* does not provide us license to act bizarre, strange, odd, abnormal, or unusual.

In fact, Charles Spurgeon explains...

> *"If we let passion take the place of judgement, and self-will reign instead of Scriptural authority, we shall fight the Lord's battles with the devil's weapons."*[70]

The devil doesn't have weapons, he has tactics.

A well-known verse regarding our spiritual warfare, Ephesians 6:10–18, reminds us to put on the full armor of God so that you and I can stand against the tactics of the Devil. It goes on to tell us that our battle is not of flesh and blood but against entities in the spiritual realms; ruling entities, authoritative entities, entities that are behind the powers of this world, and lastly, evil entities in the heavenly realm. What I find fascinating is what the apostle writes next. "So that you may be able to resist in the evil day, and having

---

[70] Spurgeon, Charles, (April 29). *Morning and Evening.* 2nd ed. Massachusetts: Hendrickson Publishers, 1991.

prepared everything, to take your stand. Stand, therefore..."[71]

Prepare to take your stand, the apostle says. He does not say to prepare to strike, prepare for ambush, or prepare to scale a wall. He says to *stand*, and stand therefore with seven essential weapons: Truth, Righteousness, Readiness of the Gospel, Faith, Salvation, the Word of God, and Prayer. In case you have not notice, these are passive weapons...only in the physical. But in the spiritual, these are the most aggressive weapons our enemy will face! Our enemy knows this all too well. Thus, the devil has forged counterfeit weapons.

Numbers 25 begins by telling us that the men of Israel began to consort with the women of Moab. Just a few chapters prior to this, we are told that the king of Moab, Balak, solicited the services a prophet named Balaam to curse the Israelites and thwarted their conquest into the promise land. However, each attempt to curse and thwarted Israel's advancement became thwarted by God's blessed covering over Israel.

Later, in Numbers 31:13–16, we read:

> *"Moses, Eleazar the priest, and all the leaders of the community went to meet*

---

[71]   Holy Bible, Ephesians 6:10–18.

> *them outside the camp. But Moses became furious with the officers, the commanders of thousands and commanders of hundreds, who were returning from the military campaign. "Have you let every female live?" he asked them. "Yet they are the ones who, at Balaam's advice, incited the Israelites to unfaithfulness against the Lord in the Peor incident, so that the plague came against the Lord's community."*[72]

As we learn through the text, Balaam was unsuccessful in cursing the nation of Israel because God had covered them under a blessing. Therefore, Balaam advises Balak to tempt Israel to sin in order to cause Israel to be removed from under the blessed covering.

Our enemy has no power over us who are in Christ. Satan has no legitimate weapons. We read in Colossians 2. 15, our enemy has been disarmed and disgraced at the cross of Christ.[73] All curses are rendered ineffective despite the rigorous efforts of hell. So, why has our enemy been so effective at afflicting and wounding us? Satan's power is in his

---

[72] Ibid., Numbers 31. 16–18.

[73] Ibid., Colossians 2.15.

ability to convincingly influence us to do contrary to what God instructs. And, if Satan can influence us to act contrary to Christ's instructions, he can cause us to be removed from Christ's blessed covering. What Satan owns are not weapons of hell but tactical forgeries of the weapons of warfare.

The Anti-Armor of Satan

Satan knows that he has no weapons of his own. But, if he can get us to use counterfeit weapons that are ineffective against him, he can effectively strike us. Instead of a belt of truth, Satan offers a girdle of "self-truth." Instead of a chest plate of righteousness, Satan offers a "medallion of high-mindedness." Instead of the sandals for readiness of the Gospel, Satan offers "boots of pleasure-seeking." Instead of a shield of faith, Satan offers a "buckler of pretentiousness." Instead of a helmet of salvation, Satan offers a "crown of good-deeds." Instead of the sword of the Word, Satan offers a "bow and arrow of self-perception." And instead of prayer, Satan offers "meditations."

Each of these offered by Satan provide a strikingly similar characteristic to its authentic original. Yet, it is a flagrant forgery. The key to Satan's tactics is found in his ability to counterfeit what God creates. Satan's works will always "...having the appearance of godliness but denying its power.

Consider the following, God's belt of truth compared to Satan's girdle of "self- truth." Proverbs 18.17 states, "The one who states his case first seems right, until the other comes and examines him."[74] The idea of "your truth" versus "my truth" holds to the principle of a lie. Keeping to "your truth" is to deny the truths that surround it. In other words, for me to believe truth is in accordance with "my truth" is to embrace that all else is a lie.

Thus, truth becomes subjective to the individual that keeps to their own truth. It, therefore, denies the truth that exists. There is no longer a standard to the truth and the truth can never be concluded. For truth to be concluded, what is *not* true must be defined. Truth is exclusive. "My truth" and "your truth" cannot be the truth at the same time unless we are saying the same thing to be true.

Consider God's chest plate of righteousness in comparison to Satan's "medallion of high-mindedness." Isaiah 64.6 states, "all our righteous deeds are like a polluted garment." Even our best efforts apart from God are polluted and corrupted.

---

[74] Ibid., Proverbs 18.17.

Satan's temptation upon us is the idea that all good deeds are godly deeds. And instead of the humility that comes with embracing the righteousness of Christ, Satan would convince us that our own nobility, our own self-righteousness that is corrupted with self-interest and selfish intent, is a form of godliness.

2 Corinthians 10.5–6, tells us, "We destroy arguments and every lofty opinion raised against the knowledge of God, and take every thought captive to obey Christ, being ready to punish every disobedience, when your obedience is complete. The danger of righteousness is that we can be easily convinced of our own high regard.

Paul's exhortation to the Corinthian church was one that targeted the spirit of pride that can easily rise up in the believer. Thus, we are all commanded to destroy, tear down, pull down, every lofty, high-minded, highly opinionated, highly exhausted idea of self and bring it into *obedience* of Christ Jesus. Moreover, this is one very thing Paul tells us to be ready to punish until it is brought to complete *obedience*.

Consider God's sandals for readiness of the Gospel in comparison to Satan's "boots of pleasure-seeking." Today, the church is guilty of teaching a Gospel of hedonism. Our pulpits are reverberating with a pleasure-seeking message instead of the Word of Jesus that is full of Grace and Truth. "Living your best life" is likened to the blessings of the Lord.

"Living your best life" is a false concept of what the Scriptures call living "Life in Abundance." The Abundant Life that God calls us to does not guarantee apartments to mansions, buses to Bentleys, and dollars to diamonds. The Abundant Life that God calls us to is likened to what we are told about Elijah, in 1 Kings 17. 8–16. According to this historical account, there was a severe famine that lasted three years in the land. In a town called, Zarephath, a widow was about to eat her final meal with her son and wait to die. However, the Lord had spoken to Elijah and prompted him to go to this women's home.

Upon his arrival, Elijah request for something to eat. The widow proceeds to explain that she had nothing left except that which she was making for her and her son. In response, the prophet tells her to make a cake for him, first, and then one for her and her son. Odd request, considering that she had just enough for one. Yet, here, Elijah is telling her to make three cakes.

As the story concludes, the widow's jars never ran out of flour or oil throughout the remaining years of the famine. Abundant life is never about the gain. It's about the never going without.

Abundant life will provide you with flour and oil in the midst of a famine. Whereas, living a life in pursuit of "your best life" seems to end in how Malcolm Muggeride once stated as, "pressing on... seeking happiness ever more ardently, and finding despair ever more abundantly."

Consider God's shield of faith in comparison to Satan's "buckler of pretentiousness." Faith is not believing the God will give you what you ask but trusting the decision God makes for you, even if it is not exactly what you have asked for. Faith is not pretentiousness. Faith informs our thought, feelings, and behaviors according to God's Word. Faith is the things hoped for and evidence of things we do not yet see.

However, faith comes only from hearing God's very Word. Faith is not believing a thing to be simply because I want to believe it will be. If what I believe is not in accordance with what God has spoken first by His Word, second by prompting of Holy Spirit, and third by aligned circumstances, chances are we are making it up. Satan is a great mentalist. He prides himself on his powers of sug-gestion and relishes opportunities to ensnare us in delusions of godliness. Let us remember this, Satan can never be accused of causing us to actu-ally commit sin.

God and sin have one thing in common, they both need us to willing commit to them.

Consider God's helmet of salvation in comparison to Satan's "crown a of good-deeds." In today's society there is an undergirding false truth rooted in the idea of a karmic balance of life. The world believes that good can adjust the bad. Conversely, there is a sub-community that comes closer to the truth then their counterparts. This sub-community believes in the balance of good and evil. Simply stated, good and evil must co-exist at an even scale. Still, this idea of truth is false.

When Eve and Adam ate from the tree of knowledge of good and evil, they became inundated with wisdom too profound for them to control. Instead, what they discovered was a heighten level of intelligence that can easily manipulate evil or selfish desires with good intentions. Such is sin. Good deeds can easily be mistaken for godly deeds. Good deeds are self-deceptive.

> *"Of all forms of deceptions, self-deception is the most deadly... the reason is simple. When a man is deceived by another, he is deceived against his will... With self-deception it is quite different. He is his own*

enemy and is working a fraud upon him-self. He wants to believe the lie and is psychologically conditioned to do so. He does not resist the deceit but collaborates with it..." [75]

- A. W. Tower

God never calls us to good deeds. He calls us to *holiness*. If they are not Holy reasons, even good reasons are not right reasons. Holiness is a sancti-tude, a sacredness, and a devotion. What holiness and the deception of good deeds have in common is a state of mind. Good deeds will be the result of Holiness, but Holiness is never produced by a good deed. Furthermore, the imputed righteous-ness of our Lord, as Franz Delitzsch stated, "is the stringency with which He acts, in accordance with the will of His holiness." All of the weapons of our warfare are predicated on the will of His holiness.

The helmet of our Salvation is the protective covering over our thought life. Salvation resides in our full belief and constitution to believing that Jesus Christ died on the cross to secure redemp-tion for a sinner, such as you and I. Our Salvation also resides in our full belief and constitution that

---

[75] Tozer, A.W. <u>Man the Dwelling Place of God.</u> Kentucky: GLH Publishing, 1966, p. 87.

what Christ says is true and all else is a lie. *"Let God be true, every one a liar..."[76]*

Salvation is worn like a helmet. Good deeds are worn like a crown. Salvation is rooted and girded in battle readiness. Good deeds are girded in exhalation and adoration. Salvation is once and for all. Good deeds are much and self-promoting. At Salvation, Christ settles it all, secures it all, and resolves it all. Good deeds continues and preserves the situation. In short, Salvation brings sin to an end. Good deeds are ongoing because it feeds on itself to produce its own desire, only to need to feed itself again.

It is the crown that was upon the heads of the twenty four elders, found in Revelations 4.10, that they all laid at the feet of Jesus in worship to him. They traded their crowns for their helmets. We, too, must lay our crowns down.

Consider God's sword of the Word in comparison to Satan's "bow and arrow of self-determination." I was once asked, "If God were a real God of love, why would there be so much suffering?" My answer was simple: God's gift of love was the gift of our own freewill. Freewill is a terribly lovely thing. God gave us the power to choose without coercion or compulsion from heaven. The true proof

---

[76] Holy Bible, Romans 3.4.

of love is in the power to choose to love or not to love. And, God has chosen to love us. However, humanity has not chosen to love Him in return. This is another ploy of Satan, self-determination.

Self-determination is the power to choose our own way, what we will believe, and how we will live out our beliefs. The tension of the "self-determined" and the Word of God comes down to one essential point. Who will have the final say? 2 Timothy 2.15 tells us, to do our best to present ourselves as one approved by God... rightly "dividing" and properly handling the Word of Truth.[77]

Wielding God's sword of the Word places a demand on submission to the Word's authority over our lives. This includes allowing the Word of God to govern our lifestyles and refusing to allow our personal idealities to govern the interpretation of God's Word.

Lastly, consider the Lord's prayer in contrast to Satan's acts of "meditation." The word of God is living and active, sharper than any two-edged sword, piercing to the division of soul and of spirit, of joints and of marrow, and discerning the thoughts and intentions of the heart. And no creature is hidden from his sight, but all are naked and

---

[77] Ibid., 2 Timothy 2.15.

exposed to the eyes of him to whom we must give account."[78]

Prayer is the active line of communication between us and God, and God and us. God's word is *active, sharp, piercing, it properly divides the real from the fake, discerning, reveals the truth of our heart, keeps nothing secrete, and makes us accountable.* "Meditation" is of another source.

Ephesians 2:2–3 tells us, "Following the course of this world, following the prince of the power of the air, the spirit that is now at work in the sons of disobedience— among whom we all once lived in the passions of our flesh, carrying out the desires of the body and the mind..."[79] The source of meditation is contemplation, consideration, pondering, and musing. Satan is the "prince of the power of the air" that works in the desires of the body and mind.

Notice the significant differences. Prayer discerns the heart, mediation works in the desires of the heart. Prayer divides between soul and spirit, what is in the nature of man from what is in the nature of God. Mediation lives in the passion of the flesh. The aestheticism of the fasting remains in the flesh if the source of fasting is not lead by

---

[78] Ibid., Hebrews 4. 12–13.

[79] Ibid., Ephesians 2. 2 -3.

Holy Spirit. The same holds true to meditation. If the source of our meditation is not rooted in God's word and driven by the prompting of the Holy Spirit, mediation is in the flesh.

Now, let us ask ourselves, why is Satan so ineffective against the armor of God? There are three principles to glean from Ephesians 6. 14 -18.

The first of these principles of our warfare is the *Given* principle. The belt of truth, a chest plate of righteousness, and the sandals for readiness of the Gospel and the helmet of Salvation are all weapons that are imputed, applied, and *given* to us through surrender to Christ. Not one of these weapons have any origin within us, nor are we capable of achieving them for ourselves. It is *Truth* that is in accordance with Christ that informs our virtues, it is the *Righteousness* of Christ that is instilled in us and enables us with a morality likened to Christ's, and it is the *Good News of Christ's gospel* that empowers us to be ready to stand up, stand fast, and step forward.

The second of these principles of our warfare is the *Grab Hold* principle. Unlike *Truth*, *Righteousness*, and the *Readiness of the Gospel*, Salvation, Faith, and the Word are weapons we must GRAB A HOLD of and act on physically. Let us remember, Salvation is described as helmet. A helmet must be put on. Although Christ has secured Salvation. Only those who grab a hold of Salvation are secured. Righteousness, we are told, is how we shall live and we shall live it by Faith. Faith is also the substance of our hope in Christ. Moreover, Faith comes only by hearing the word of God. And the Word is our sword. Observe how these weapons are interlocked to one another. We receive Salvation by Faith. Faith comes by hearing God's word and by faith we believe the very word of God.

The third of these principles of our warfare is the *Grow Aware* principle. "Pray at all times," Paul says. "Stay alert," he follows up. Prayer is our spiritual communication with God, prayer is our spiritual optics into the realm of the supernatural, and prayer is our only action taken *against* our enemy.

There is a moment in all of our lives when we must stop moving from one experience to the next and just *"stand"* on our truthful experience with *"the God of whom we belong."* Knowing the God of the others is not enough.

Chapter 10

PREDESTINED, NOT PREDETERMINED

. . . .

S emantics...a word commonly used within the church community to condescendingly imply that someone is in disagreement with our own understanding of a subject. It is also a term used to describe someone when the other desires to dismiss a discussion they seek to avoid because they are afraid to admit that they may not have a full knowledge of a subject, or that they don't understand the subject at all. I, myself, have been accused of being semantical. And to all of my accusers, I have offered this one question. Was God being semantical when He declared you saved, delivered, set free, healed, or restored? In fact, I find it quite contrary to the truth when we in the church chalk-up serious issues to semantics, when semantics is actually the practice for searching out true meaning.

Do you know the context in which Jesus states, "You will know the truth and the truth will set you free?"[80] Jesus made this statement in the context of submission to His discipleship. It kind of changes the idea of being set free, doesn't it? True freedom cannot be actualized until we are in complete submission to a life in Christ. The freedom that we may find in knowing the truth is only contingent upon our concerted efforts to participate with Holy Spirit in truth that is only found in Jesus.

Philosophically speaking, finding the meaning to our lives is an act of semantics. Depending on how one determines what is the truth, one will define one's life course. Thus, it is imperative to find the true meaning for life. But how does one find life's true meaning, when difficult times in life appears to be prearranged and already intended?

Times of difficulty easily entrap us into thinking about who we are and in what direction we may be going. Times of difficulty easily entrap us into reflective thinking about what has happened, what could have happened, what should have happened, and what would have happened, as opposed to asking ourselves, what

---

[80] Holy Bible., John 8.32.

can I help happen from what I learned from what has happened?

Moreover, times of difficulty make it easy for us to buy into the idea that things may be pre-arranged. Let's face it, it's easier to romanticize the idea that what has resulted in our lives during great trails is prearranged and firmly fixed prior to existence. As opposed to dealing with the harsh truth that life is a collection of varying wills colliding simultaneously, while the will of God remains unmoved by our unwillingness to follow His will.

A.R. Bernard once said, "God did not design us to die but to live." Yet, we experience death. Matthew 25:41 reads, "...eternal fire [was] prepared for the devil and his angels." Yet, many of us will experience hell fire and be absent in heaven. How then is this so?

Predestined not Predetermined

Human life is not predetermined. All human life possesses an unconditional predestination. This is not to be confused with the dogmatic arguments deliberating on whether or not the election of a particular individual is conditional upon faith in Christ verses the notion of an unconditional election. It is true to say that our choices are predetermined, in that, ultimately, they all narrow down to only two of life's choices; believe Christ and all that He says or don't believe Christ and own up to its end results. Even still, you and I are not predetermined. We are predestined.

Jeremiah 1, reads, "Before I formed you in the womb I knew you, and before you were born, I consecrated you."[81] To God, all human life is consecrated. To God...*life is consecrated.*

What an overwhelming truth. God knew you and I *before* we were ever conceived; before our parents consummated their relationship to produce us. He knew us by name, even! Yet, God does not stop there. He proceeds to *consecrate* you and I before birth. Here is what we need to understand when He says He consecrates us before we were born.

Before birth, God dedicated, devoted, gave, set aside, assigned, allotted, allocated, reserved, consigned, pledged, vowed, offered, surrendered, sacrificed, and sanctified every aspect pertaining to our lives for the sustainability and longevity of our life's existence. Can you see now how even the most outrageous and despicable individual can live a rich full life despite such a lifestyle? Before God formed us in the womb, He knew us and consecrated us.

---

[81] Ibid., Jeremiah 1.4-5.

> *"God created us out of love...Scripture proclaims that this love, from which and for which we are created, is perfect...it draws us toward itself by means of our own deepest desires...this love wants us to have free will... We are intended to make free choices... we are not puppets or automatons... Spiritually, our freedom allows us to choose as we wish for or against God, life, and love... free will is given to us for a purpose: so that we may choose freely, without coercion or manipulation, to love God in return, and to love one another in a similar and perfect way."*[82]

> *- Gerald G. May*

You and I are not born determined to go to hell. If so, God could not maintain that He is a just God. He would then need to take moral accountability for who we were determined to be before we became. God could not assert himself as a Just God if He were to *punish* you or I for being what He predetermined us to be before we were.

If this were characteristic of God, God would be a petty, superficial, an imperfect being who

---

[82] May, Gerald, p. 13.

views humanity as nothing more than play things. Additionally, should our lives be predetermined heaven would be empty. "All have sinned and fallen short of the Glory of God."

In Psalm 35 we read, "Great is the Lord, who delights in the welfare of his servant!"[83] Hellfire is not of great welfare. And here, we find that God *delights* in human welfare; especially the welfare of those whose lives have become undeniably devoted to Him. It is further clear that the nuance within this verse is that of a servant.

The servant is the one who inclines themselves to service, to carrying out assigned duties, and intentionally inclines themselves to the instructions of whom they serve. This is a chosen act of service, not to be confused with a fixed unconscious behavior. Such is the case between predestination and predetermination. Predestination is not to be confused with Predetermination.

> *Let us not make the mistake of believing that God chooses our final destination. God has just set a course. It is up to us to decide where we will end up.*

---

[83]   Holy Bible, Psalm 35:27.

Jesus tells us "Enter through the narrow gate, because the gate is wide and the way is spacious that leads to destruction. And there are many who enter through it. But the gate is narrow, and the way is difficult that leads to life, and there are few who find it."[84]

Here lies three alarming truths to behold. First, the gate that is the entrance to destruction is wide and easily entered. Second, many enter it. In other words, the wide gate is so unassuming and appears seemingly harmless. Therefore, it is easily and mistakenly entered. We should not be so impudent and full of ego as to think that we are the only exceptions. Lest we forget, there is a third and final truth to be gleaned here. The narrow gate is one that only *few* will find.

> *"All the activity of the disciples is subject to the clear precept of their Lord. They are not left free to choose their own methods or adopt their own conceptions of their task. Their work is to be Christ-work, and therefore they are absolutely dependent on the will of Jesus... The work of God*

---

[84] Ibid., Matthew 7:13–14.

> *cannot be done without due authorization, otherwise it is devoid of promise."*[85]

- Dietrich Bonhoeffer

Narrow is the gate and very few find it. This is a harsh reality for some of us in the church to grasp because we are a people riddled with "good intentions." Paradoxically, it is those very "good intentions" that keep us from finding the narrow gate. Our predestination has very little and nothing to do with who we are as people. On the contrary, our predestination has *everything* to do with what *path* we choose to take and how we proceed along the path.

Predestination can be best described as an interstate highway where, at each end of that highway, lies a pre-established destination. Now, where you or I end up is entirely based upon the direction we choose to head towards. The destinations are already preset. You and I, however, choose which of those destinations we will ultimately arrive. Similarly, God has pre-established two destinations for our life's journey. Yet, it is up to you and I who decide which of those destinations we will get to.

---

[85] Bonhoeffer, Dietrich, "The Cost of Discipleship," New York: Touchstone, 1959, P. 206.

As Jesus describes, the wide gate is one that is easily entered. At the wide gate there are no restrictions of how to enter, no contingencies along the way, and no means in accordance with its end. And although the gate is wide, it is easy to be tricked into because of our ability to Christianize our activities.

Take, for example, reasoning "for the greater good." To reason action "for the greater good" is not a kingdom principle nor a practice. Our Good Shepherd, Jesus Christ, thinks opposite of this principle. He leave ninety-nine (the greater) for the one (the least). Jesus referred to the least as great in His kingdom. Lastly, Christ volunteered His own life and died for all sinners and not just for the sins of some. In contrast, reasoning "for the greater good" is devoid of the voluntary action one takes in laying down their life freely. Reasoning "for the greater good" justifies the condemning of one's life while denying them the right to make the choice to surrender it.

Our greatest misconception of Jesus' substitutionary sacrifice is the assumption that because only some will attain eternal life, Christ's death was a propitious act for few. We seem to forget that eternal life is contingent upon our willful admission of our guilt, acceptance, and receiving of Christ Jesus as Lord and Savior, and a lifestyle consistent with repentance.

Another example of how we can easily be tricked into entering the wide gate is the idea of "the ends justify the means." In his commentary about the 40 days of temptations, Tasker stated, "Jesus was, in effect, tempted to subscribe to the diabolical doctrine that the end justifies the means.[86] If you will look into Matthew 4, you will notice that Satan never attempts to cause Jesus doubt about His Sonship to the Father. In fact, Satan continually affirms this fact by stating, "If you are the Son of God." Satan's attempt to tempt Jesus was to suggest that Jesus had every right and entitlement to satisfy His own needs. Everyone needs to recognize and acknowledge his or her total dependence on God and His Word. Jesus' real food – what sustained Him above all else – was His commitment to do the will of His Father.[87]

---

[86] Tasker, R. V. G. The Gospel According to St. Matthew: An Introduction and Commentary. Tyndale New Testament Commentaries series. Grand Rapids: Wm. B. Eerdmans Publishing Co., 1961.

[87] Constable, Thomas L. https://www.planobiblechapel. org/tcon/notes/html/nt/matthew/matthew.htm

"Obedience to God's will takes priority over self-gratification, even over the apparently essential provision of food."[88]

Our faith in Christ must be followed by our function in Christ. The ends do not justify the means by which we function. The means are pre-requisite to the ends. It is the narrow gate that sets the destination for eternal life and never our desire for eternal life that determines the gate. God has never failed in giving instructions for what He intends. For instance, Noah was told to build an ark. What Noah was not told was to build the ark based on his own ingenuity. Instead, God provides Noah with a clear and concise blue-print for how He would have Noah built this ark. God, also, included instructions for who He would have Noah take and how many of each animal He would allow.

When God called Moses to be the deliverer of Israel, He provided Moses with clear instruction on how to approach Pharaoh. During the plagues, God provided Moses with clear instructions on how the Israelites should protect themselves. While in the desert, God provided Moses with Ten Commandments – clear instructions – for

---

[88] Ibid., https://www.planobiblechapel.org/tcon/notes/html/nt/matthew/matthew.htm

how the Israelites should conduct themselves as a community of people separated onto Himself. Again, predestination is not about the persons but about the path and the path comes complete with instruction.

> **God is not an elitist. He shows no partiality but anyone who fears him and does what is right is acceptable to him.**

In contrast, 2 Thessalonians 2.10–12 tells us, "every kind of evil deception directed against those who are perishing, because they found no place in their hears for the truth so as to be saved. Consequently, God sends on them a deluding influence so that they will believe what is false. And so, all of them who have not believed the truth but have delighted in evil will be condemned.[89]

Here is the daunting truth. Every evil deception is directed towards those who "are perishing." But why are they perishing is the question? As we read forward, we discover the answer. "Because they found no place in their hearts for the truth so as to be saved." Because they have found *no place* in their hearts for the truth, they *choose* the lie and they therefore are not saved.

---

[89] Holy Bible., 2 Thess. 2. 10-12.

To entertain a lie is to deny the truth, and refusal to believe what is true is to endorse the lie. Moreover, to refuse to be saved according to the truth, is to accept the loss of your soul. Thus, God cannot be held morally responsible for our choice to deny him, refuse him, reject him.

Acts 17:26–27, 30 states, "He made from one man every nation of mankind to live on all the face of the earth, having determined allotted periods and the boundaries of their dwelling place, that they should seek God, and perhaps feel their way toward him and find him. Yet he is actually not far from each one of us... The times of ignorance God overlooked, but now he commands all people everywhere to repent..."[90]

Observe, God determined allotted periods and the boundaries. Now compare this to, "they should seek God, and perhaps feel their way toward him and find him." God has set a course but we choose the direction we will go. Again, it is our decision where we will end up.

Lastly, consider what we are told in Acts 19:8–9 when Paul and Barnabas entered a synagogue and for three months "spoke boldly, reasoning and persuading them about the kingdom

---

[90] Ibid., Acts 12. 26-27, 30.

of God."[91] Yet, the Scripture tells us that some of the members chose to become stubborn and continued in unbelief.

Paul and Barnabas were in the church preaching and teach of Christ's way, truth, and life. They were offering this community the gospel of Jesus and an opportunity to receive eternal life. To be clear, these were church people, not people of the world. However, Scripture tells us *"They became stubborn."* This is a choice and not a predetermination. Scripture also says, *"they continued in disbelief."* This is also a choice and not a predetermination. Becoming is an active choice, continuing is an active choice. What active choices are we making?

This should cause us all to be found with a level of godly fear that is reverential toward this admonishment of good faith. And in good faith, Christ stated these words to those He knew would hear and hear what the Spirit of the Lord was speaking. I would further like to add that Christ described this narrow gate in the context of speaking with His disciples.

Now why is this such an important piece of information to know? It is important because where predetermination would tell us what will

---

[91]   Ibid., Acts 19. 8-9.

be is what was always meant to be, predestination tells us what to do to get where we need to go.

Another great misconception of ours is to delineate predetermination based on God's foreknowledge. Looking back at the analogy of the narrow gate, we see that Christ describes Himself as the narrow gate. Christ's description of Himself as the narrow gate was indicative of His ability to see who would enter through Him. But more clearly, watching for who would follow through on His invitation to enter. I can have a foreknowledge of your coming to my home but our fellowship will not be actualized until you actually enter in my house.

Predestination is not about selected persons, it's about the person's selection. The narrow gate is the entry way towards a pathway that leads to eternal life. Christ is the way. In other words, predestination is about our responsiveness towards Christ's invitation to a lifestyle becoming of Him. Thus, Christ becomes our standard of living. But also, Christ becomes our limitation. Narrow is the gate.

Conversely, the limitations we find in Christ are actually freedoms. When we adhere to this narrow walkway, we soon become free of all our estimations, projections, and guess work. We can now lean on assurances, comforts, peace, and rest provided by our Lord because it is His pathway. Psalm 37:23–24 tells us, "The steps of a man are established by the Lord, when... that man delights in God's way."[92] It is the Lord's way that is established for us when the Lord's way becomes our great joy and pleasure to partake in.

Lastly, let us remember that Christ tells us in John 10, "I am the door... *Anyone who enters* through me shall have eternal life. I came so they may have life..."

We are PREDESTINED toward life.
PREDETERMINATION always ends in death.

---

92 Ibid., Psalm 37:23–24.

Chapter 11

BACK TO START

· ·

The sign read, "Caution, road conditions ahead." Reading these words upon the electronic screen was enough for my mind to drift into introspective thought while I eased my right foot off the gas pedal and adjusted my speed to avoid any potential dangers before me. It was already several hours into a seventeen-hour drive, south bound. I was on my way to gather my belongings from a place I once called home. My now ex-wife was found committing a hurtful act against our marriage. But more importantly, she created scenarios to surround this egregious act and keep me distracted from what was occurring.

The yellow lights seemed to place me under a form of hypnosis as my mind was carried away into a slow current of memories reflecting the incidents that lead me behind the steering wheel of my vehicle towards another windy path of my journey. I could not help becoming inundated by the emotions attached to each eventuality experienced along the way. As my mind fast-forwarded through the various scenes within the living script of my life, each event that lead to this moment was all perplexed by one question, "Why?"

The question appeared to echo through the hollows of my by brain. This event left me despondent, confused, and questioning my walk of faith. Then a voice, in the form of whisper, breathed these words in my mind. "Ray, do you love me unconditionally?" In an instance, my defenses went up and I become entangled with a wrestling within my spirit. I heard the voice again. "Ray, do you love me unconditionally?" Realizing this was the Lord, I started to think of the right answer. There is only one right answer and God knows it. Thus, I found solace in the words of the apostle Peter, and I replied, "Lord you know."

Holy Spirit, in His gentleness begins to take a different approach. "Ray, I love you unconditionally, so when will you begin to love me without conditions?" In this instant I realized much of our relationship to God is based on, contingent upon, determined by, hinges on, subjected to, and under the *conditions* of whatever we place before Him that ultimately serves to our benefit.

Holy Spirit then proceeded to explain...

"Consider my relationship to you. I chose my relationship with you regardless of what I knew about you and even before entering into the relationship with you. I knew what I would be getting into coming into the relationship. Yet, I still chose to be in relationship with you. I knew about the good of you, I knew about the bad of you, and I knew about the ugly of you. Yet, I still chose you. It was not about you deserving the relationship, it is about me choosing a relationship with you. My love is unconditional. So now, can you be willing to continue in a relationship with me regardless of what decisions I make without argument or without conditions?"

There are conditions on the road ahead. God establishes the conditions, and we must accept these conditions without our own conditions in reciprocity. Moreover, God's unconditional love does not mean He does not make a demand for better. What it does mean is that He does not leave us, even if we fail. In contrast, we are likely to leave Him when we believe He has failed us.

The same way God does not make conditions for who could ask for him to

***save them, He desires that we would
not make conditions for how He will do
the saving.***

To best understand this characteristic of God's unconditional love, we would need to understand the analogy of Christ and the church as the Bridegroom and the Bride.

This is a Profound Mystery; Christ's love.

In his closing argument about the conduct of marriage, Paul states, "This mystery is profound. I am saying that it refers to Christ and the Church."[93] Paul's view of marriage was one of being God-ordained. More importantly, Paul viewed marriage as being analogous to the union between Christ and His eternal love and commitment to the Church.

Did you know that there are approximately three hundred sixty eight verses in the Bible about marriage? Of which, 25% of the 50% of the New Testament written by Paul, address the issue of marriage. Moreover, of the three hundred sixty eight verses written about marriage, approximately 25 of them specifically prohibit divorce.

---

[93]   Ibid., Ephesians 5.32.

Let's do the math. Of three hundred sixty eight verses in the Bible on marriage, only 25 are about divorce. What this tells us is that marriage and the commitment of marriage is a big deal to God.

*Scripture is very clear about **defining what determines whether or not divorce is the only option for a marriage or if divorce is being used as a means to an easy and sinful way out of a commitment of marriage.***

Dr. Thomas Constable writes:

"In our day, one popular way to deal with marriage problems is to split up, and this has always been an attractive option for many people. Nevertheless, the Lord's will is that all people, including believers, work through their marital problems—rather than giving up on them by separating permanently... If separation (divorce) occurs ("if she does leave"), they should ("she must") "remain unmarried" (i.e., stay

as they are), "or else be reconciled" with their mate."[94]

It is impossible for a Christian husband and or a Christian wife to be a testimony of Christ's forgiveness and reconciliation if they cannot forgive and reconcile with their Christian husband or wife. Moreover, Paul consistently rejects the notion that the married may dissolve their marriages... What he did not want was for believers to initiate the termination of their marriages, just for any reason.[95]

There are two important chapters in Scripture pertaining to marriage; Ephesians 5 and 1 Corinthians 7. Where, Ephesians 5 provides us a correct view for what we need to do in our marriages. 1 Corinthians 7 offers us a clear view of what we need *not* be doing in our marriages. For example:

---

[94] Constable, Thomas L. https://www.planobiblechapel.org/tcon/notes/html/nt/1corinthians/1corinthians.htm

[95] Fee, Gordon D. The First Epistle to the Corinthians. New International Commentary on the New Testament series. Grand Rapids: Wm. B. Eerdmans Publishing Co., 1987.

1. Retaining our "exclusive personal rights." Paul admonishes us from withholding ourselves from those we are married to.

2. Physical Abuse. Paul explains that God calls us to "Peace." In the use of the example of being married to a "non-believer," the nuance indicates preventing the disruption of the marriage union that is called to love, joy, peace, patience, kindness, gentleness, faithfulness, goodness, and *self-control*.

3. Prohibiting marriage to an *unbeliever*. Again, the idea, here, is to prevent being in a disruptive and contentious relationship especially on the principle of one's own beliefs.

4. Infidelity.

Jesus Christ was once asked this very question, "Is it lawful for a man to divorce his wife on *any* grounds?" Christ's reply was clear. "Moses permitted this because of the *hardness of your heart*. But this was not what God *intended* at the beginning." Christ, then, states His position on the matter. Whoever (both men and women) divorces, except for marital unfaithfulness and marries another commits adultery."[96]

Let us be clear, marriage has conditions, and those conditions are not ours to place, those conditions belong to God and God alone.

Marriage is a God-Breathed institution. But before God would establish this institution, God needed to define the parameters by which this institution could properly function. The first parameter God establishes is who could participate in this institution. "When God created humanity, He made them in His likeness. Male and female, He created them and He blessed them."[97]

Genesis 5. 1–2, compared with Genesis 1.26, provides us with a perspicuous detail to understanding, what is, the first parameter in this institution. All humanity was created in God's image and in God's likeness. In other words, we possess tangible aspects of God as well as intangible aspects of God. Being born in the image of God reflects the tangible.

---

[96]   Holy Bible, Matthew 19.3–8.

[97]   Ibid., Genesis 5.1–2.

Christ, when speaking to His disciples about prayer and asking for gifts, says to them, "if you then, who are evil, know how to give good gifts to your children, how much more will the Heavenly Father give the Holy Spirit to those who ask him!"[98] The tangible of God can be seen here. Those who are evil know how to give good gifts. God is good. Yet even evil people, who are created in God's image can act in kindness or good. This is a reflection of the tangible image of God. However, this is not a reflection of the intangible or the *likeness* of God.

The likeness of God can be best understood through what Paul tells us in Ephesians 1.11. "In Him we have obtained an inheritance, having been predestined according to the purpose of Him...". In other words, all of our self-absorbed, self-intended, self-motivated, and selfish purposes are now outweighed by what God proposes. Unlike God's image that possesses outward beauty, the very inner reflection of God's likeness becomes His character in us. The likeness of God shapes our Christian lives as all of our personal realizations, traditions of truth, cultural influences become filtered through the strainer of Scripture. Whatever

---

[98] Ibid., Luke 11.13.

enters into the filter of God becomes cleaned, cleared, and corrected for the purposing of God.

Thus, when God stated that Adam and Eve were created in His *likeness,* God instituted established a holy union with meaningful purpose. All relationships thereafter would be qualified and defined by it. God had an intentional motive for designing a male and female. And God blesses them (us) as they are found functioning in the purposeful order by which He intended for them. Many of us are found in God's image but we are not functioning in His likeness.

The Calling comes first before the ministry.

Eve and Adam's grave mistake in the garden were two. They did not trust God's intentions for them when He gave them restrictions in the garden. And because they did not trust God's intentions for them, they were not faithful to the assignments that God designated specifically to them.

If you observe the events in Genesis 1–3, you will see that before God formed Eve, Adam was given an assignment. Adam was tasked the duty naming the animals according to their functions. However, prior to this event, God makes a declaration for both Eve and Adam that they would have dominion over all that occupies the earth. Remember, Eve had not yet been called to existence. Thus, what God establishes for Eve and Adam was a *calling*. Adam had received a calling and now was given a job. God then provides Adam a wife. Before Adam had a first ministry, God gave Adam a first calling.

Adam's calling was onto God. Prior to meeting Eve, Adam's priority was towards God and what God had assigned to him. Now here lies the rub. When we read Genesis 3, we find an operational malfunction. Eve was tending a tree that was on the list of prohibitions and Adam was there watching. Operational malfunction: Genesis 2.18 tells us, "The Lord said it is not good that the man should be alone; I will make a helper fit for him." Eve's assigned task was Adam's help. Yet, in Genesis 3, we find Eve doing Adam's job. Easy target for the enemy. Why? They had already disturbed the divine arrangement of the Lord and subjected themselves to the execrable schemes of the devil.

Never in Scripture do we read, "a man's marriage is his first ministry." What we do read, however, is "He must manage his own household well, with all dignity... for if someone does not know how to manage his own household, how will he care for God's church?"[99] Dignity is only found in the likeness of God. Thus, if a man does not have the calling of God first, he will never be able to manage the ministry of his home.

The parameters of marriage are marked clearly throughout Scripture. Proverbs 18.22 says, "He who finds a wife finds a good thing and obtains flavor from the Lord."[100] Take note, that it is he who finds a "wife." It is *"wife"* as *defined* by God. It is in accordance with that very definition that, he who does find a wife finds God's favor. The favor that is found with finding a wife is finding a wife as she is defined by God.

The same holds true for a husband. Anyone of us that does not operate in accordance with how God defines, describes, and distinguishes what a wife is, or what God defines, describes, and distinguishes as a husband is nothing more than a spouse.

> ***God never describes a spouse.***
> ***He distinguishes what is a husband***
> ***and a wife.***

---

[99]   Ibid., 1 Timothy 3. 4–5.

[100]   Ibid., Proverbs 18.22.

Road Conditions

The biggest lie that the church defines as a doctrinal truth is "Agreeing to Disagree." Agreeing to disagree is to put asunder what God put together. Agreeing to disagree is to embrace coming apart. In short, many of our Christian relationships have become practitioners of "Putting Asunder" what God has put together. What God has put together let *no one* put asunder. Teaching that it is okay to agree to disagree is teaching *dividing and departing* and not the *reconciling and returning*. Is there any wonder why the church is so divided?

If we would take a look at our Christian homes, we will find the proof of the fruit that makes known what is of God and what is not. And much of what is found in our Christian homes, today, would be categorized as "what is not of God." As a rhetorical question, God speaks through the prophet, Amos, and asks the community of Judah, "Can two walk together unless in agreement?"[101] The question was intended to elicit an emphatic "No," as the prophet attempted to stir the hearts of the community towards coming back to God.

G.K. Chesterton once said...

---

[101] Ibid., Amos 3.3.

"I have known many happy marriages, but never a compatible one. The whole aim of marriage is to fight through and survive the instant when incompatibility becomes unquestionable."[102]

Many marriages have forgotten how to set aside their exclusive rights and humble themselves to the authority of Scripture. In order for our Christian relationship to succeed, we must agree to allow Scripture to overrule our rules. If Christian relationships would trade in the practice of "Agreeing to Disagree," the practice of putting asunder, in exchange for "Walking together in Agreement," we would experience a enormous drop in the number of divorces experienced in the church.

The practice of "Walking together in Agreement" is the practice of looking at our disagreements comparatively with the word of God. Too many of us make demands for a supernatural change in our relationships. Yet, we do not make a demand to the practical changes we can make by simply following the instructions found tangibly written in the Bible.

When we change the way we think for how God thinks, when we trust in God's intentions for us over our own self-seeking intention the world

---

[102] http://biblereasons.com/marriage/

around us does not change, He changes the world within us. It is sad how much of the world we still trust in and believe in. It is sad how much of the world is still within who we are Christians.

Unfortunately, Scripture advises us that in our days many will become lovers of themselves. They will become intolerant of sound doctrine. Having itchy ears, they will gather for themselves teachers; preachers who would teach and preach estates that would appease their own passions.[103] Jesus warned us that there will be a time when members of our own families would become our enemies.[104]

The fact is that my ex-wife did not get what she wanted and rejected what God was providing. That "missing" became the justification by which she would chase after what and whom she believed would give her what she "desired" for herself, and "give up" what God had "destined" for her.

The mansion is the curse if the shack is where God's blessings reside. Christ chose to reside in the manger. He found no place at the inn.

---

[103] Holy Bible, 2 Timothy 3. 1, 4. 3-4.

[104] Ibid., Mark 13. 1–13.

When we learn to "Walk together in Agreement," we learn how to fight *for* each other and stop fighting *with* each other. "What God puts together let no one put asunder." The issues of pornography, disrespect, micro-aggressions, insecurity, financial difficulties, and generational pathologies no longer are viewed as the bane of our relationships, and become viewed as the targets of our prayers.

In God, there are no perfect relationships except the one we possess with Him. God takes imperfect people and makes purposeful relationships. Perfect relationships have no place for the imperfections of people within them. When we become engaged in the purposefulness of our relationships, we learn how to *pray* for each other's weaknesses, not *prey* on each other's weaknesses.

Our enemy comes like a roaring lion seeking prey that he would devour. Our enemy comes to rob, kill, and destroy. Our enemy seeks opportunities to rob from us in the physical – kill us in the psychological – so he can destroy us in the spiritual. Lastly, our enemy seeks for one of us to become complicit to the robbing, killing, and destroying. This is the principle idea behind Ephesians 5 and 1 Corinthians 7. Paul emphasized the *staying* and not the leaving, the reconciling and returning, and not the dividing and departing.

Returning to the Eve and Adam experience, we see that when Eve and Adam forgot their place, they lost their purpose. Whether you can accept this or not, Genesis 3 is where we witness the first divorce. Eve and Adam had become separated; divorced, from God. The consequences of the separation and divorce has caused everyone to suffer.

The consequences of separation and divorce were so severe that the impact of the separation persisted until Eve and Adam gave birth to a son named Seth. But it is until Seth gives birth to his own son, Enosh, that people began to call upon the name of the Lord again. These are the results of the consequences of separation. Adam lost two sons until the age of 130 when Eve gave birth to Seth. At 105 years of age, Seth finally has a son named Enosh. And it was until Enosh that the name of the Lord was called upon, again. Put this into perspective. For 235 years, God was not present. For 235 years, they were lost and without a purpose.

Marriage is a God-designed institution. Marriage is not – nor ever was – a worldly construct. God defines what marriage is; how it is to be established; the role each husband and wife must take; and how they are to function. This is the mystery of marriage as it is analogous to Christ and the Church: "Through the church, the manifold wisdom of God might be made know..."[105] Marriage is intended to be a tangible reflection of the manifold wisdom of God's forgiveness, fortitude, reconciliation, redemption, sacrifice, and service. If we do not embrace this truth, we will never truly embrace the exclusivity and divine establishment of marriage between a woman and a man.

Moreover, denial of this divine arrangement will be to deny Christ's husband-hood and the church's bride-hood. Lastly, this divine arrangement is not gender biased to the functions of marriage, these are gender *specific* functions of marriage.

Christ came to serve. The church was intended to yield to the serving will of Christ. Husbands cannot serve a wife who cannot yield to his service. The church is called to submit. Christ calls Himself to love the church. Wives cannot submit to a husband who will not love in accordance with the love of Christ. The service is not just any type of service. The service is clearly described and is a service that serves instructionally. More specifically, these gender specific functions hold moral responsibilities towards one to the other. Lastly, marriage is intended towards three purposes:

---

[105] Ibid., Ephesians 3.10.

1. Marriage is supposed to last a lifetime. Christ offers life and life eternally.

2. Marriage is supposed to be as God's intended. Christ has predestined us to be in accordance with His image and His likeness.

3. Marriage is supposed to model the great model of reconciliation. Christ voluntarily dies on a cross so that we could be reconciled to God.

Can two walk together unless they agree?

The damage caused to my relationship with my ex-wife was not one-sided. Much of the emotional hurt I caused her during my intermittent bouts with pornography and drinking still haunt me to this day, and with great pain. The expressions of agony that formed on her face is still etched into my memories. However, the pain of being blamed, years after overcoming my bouts; being reminded that I was only as good as my last fall; and never being credited for the accomplished strides I made through the power of the Holy Spirit have caused me an equal share of pain.

God never provides us with a day by day, or play by play detailed account for any of the personalities found in the Bible. God does, however, give us clear direct detailed instructions on how we are to behave, act, and function. Our failure to follow His clear instruction is a clear indication of our failure to believe God. The church is guilty of being filled with believing non-believers.

Consequently, my relationship with my ex-wife suffered from not "Walking in Agreement." Our commitment and fidelity to God and His definition of marriage were of two different ideals. I desired to seek the agreement of two to walk together. She insisted that she wanted the "right" to disagree. Two Christians cannot walk together in marriage unless they agree that God's definitions of what is pertaining to the marriage is absolute and unequivocally correct. Let what God says always be true and all of what we say be *false*.[106]

Six months prior to our separation, my ex-wife and I were told of a dream a dear sister in the Lord had pertaining to our marriage. She shared that in her dream, my ex-wife threw me out of our house because of a table she did not want. She further explained that my ex-wife became hostile and sent into fire. Lastly, she explained that my good friend and Senior Pastor was seen sleeping on our couch while this was occurring.

---

[106] Ibid., Romans 3.4.

Later that day, my ex-wife and I had a discussion about this dream. I had asked her to remain prayerful and conscientious about why and what we found ourselves fighting over. I, also, asked her to promise me that she would never kick me out but that she would work through the issues with me. She, in turn, told me that I was being paranoid and that she would never do such a thing. Unfortunately...all that the dream revealed came to pass.

While on a trip to visit my family, my ex-wife decided that she no longer desired to be married to me and suggested I stay with my family. A couple of months after that, I was told by a leader in our church, where I was the Assistant Pastor, that my wife had been seen with another person. They further stated that the event was told to the Senior Pastor, who told them to ignore it.

As time passed, I found myself reading Scripture and asking God for clarity about the struggles I was experiencing my relationship to my ex-wife. There, I came across Romans 11. 8–9, which reads, "God gave them a spirit of stupor, eyes that would not see and ears that would not hear, down to this very day... Let their *table* become a snare and a trap, a stumbling block and a retribution for them; let their eyes be darkened so that they cannot see..."[107]

Psalm 23.5 tells us, "You prepare a *table* before me in the presence of my enemy; you anoint my head with oil; my cup overflow."[108] When we refuse the *table* God sets for us in exchange for the *table* we desire, our *table* eventually becomes a snare and trap. God does not make suggestions. He is faithful to His word and stands by His word. Even when there is doubt, God will confirm His word with a confirming message, a confirming messenger, or even a confirming dream. Again, let what God says always be true and all of what we say be *false*.

There is a danger to self-motivated interpretations of God's word. Self-motivated interpretations of God's word and seeing truth through a quantitative lens is always subject to the gentry, popular consensus, and self-righteous motivations. Quantitative truth only allows us to see some portion of the truth while denying the veracity of the whole of truth. This portion of the truth is normally the portion that is to our own advantage.

Furthermore, quantitative truth disqualifies the fullness of God's true reasoning in your experiences. Yet, truth in accordance with our Lord is

---

[107] Ibid., Romans 11. 8–9.

[108] Ibid,. Psalm 23.5.

always consistent with itself and contains congruent coherency that paints the picture for the use of truth's consistency. And God's truth has a remarkable way of speaking the truth in such a way that we are without doubt to what He is truly saying.

we are told, in Genesis 4, that Adam and Eve ad two sons by the names of Cain and Abel. We further read that both brothers presented offerings onto God. Abel's offer was accepted. However, Cain's offering was not acceptable. As we continue to read, Cain became angered. Yet, of the two individuals, God chooses to speak privately to Cain. In this conversation, God advises Cain that if he would offer what was asked of him instead of what he thought was good enough to offer, God would acceptance his offering. However, this advice was not acceptable to Cain. And instead of changing his methods, Cain decides to change his relationship and kills his brother.

We are like Cain in many ways. We have many difficulties accepting what God calls appropriate, acceptable, and awardable. Like Cain, we want to decide what is okay to offer God. We love to make our own way to God. We insist on having our own mediums, methods, and materials. Even in our best of intentions if good is not of God, our good is still evil.

We are like Cain in our prayer lives, as well. We demand to speak freely and get freely of God. Yet, we place conditions for how God will speak and what we will take from God. We want to "customize" our relationships with God. What we don't want is to submit to God's customs. In the end, God is not really our God, and we are still the lords of our lives.

In our journeying and walk with God, there are road conditions that we will need to adjust and conform to in order to make our way. When we commit to Christ, we are no longer in a position to demand what road we take, nor the rules of the road we will abide by. He sets the course, and He gives us the rules of the road.

God accepts us unconditionally. Yet, God wants us to accept His ways without conditional, as well. This is the entirety of meaning behind "Trust in the Lord with all of your hearts, and do not lean on your own understanding. In all your ways acknowledge him, He will make straight your paths."[109] The road toward God's way, His truth, and His life has conditions. Our unconditional acceptance does not include actions with impunity. God establishes the conditions, and we must accept them unconditionally.

---

[109] Ibid., Proverbs 3.5–6.

At the Bend

As I drove through the long winding night, I began to pose a question before God. "Lord," I asked, "is it that I have relationship issues?" His reply startled me. "Yes, you do...Do you not realize that your relationship to me will always be the issue? However, Ray, that agonizing love that you still hold on to for someone who loves you no more, is exactly the same feelings of love I hold for those that turn away and choose not to love me." Tears began to pour out from my eyes as I began to pray...

> *"Dear Lord, Hell's clever little ruse for stealing my marriage has only succeeded in giving my the fury of heaven and burns with desire to go and steal the hell out of marriages. Thus, I will set my heart like a flint, dig y feet deep in the foundations of your Truth, and press forward. For the lose of one marriage, I ask, to take back thousands, for two, ten thousand. God, if you will, take this mess and use if for you miracle. In Jesus name, Amen!"*

Chapter 12

THE REAR
VIEW MIRROR

. . . .

W isdom is like the rear view mirror of a car. It allows us to see in hindsight. Yet, it does not keep us simply retrospective or backward-looking. The beauty of a rear-view mirror is this: what remains on the back end slowly becomes smaller until it dissolves into the rear canvas, while we are proceeding forward towards the newer horizon. Wisdom means we have learned from the past and have gained the knowledge and understanding to move forward. Otherwise, we would still be at the back end of the road. Lastly, the rear-view mirror does not keep us looking back, it helps us to fix our eyes looking ahead.

Looking into the rear-view mirror of my life you will see the obscurity, uncertainty, fear, false ideal-ities, and lofty romanticisms of what a life in Christ is like. I took many losses because of these false opinions of my Christianity. I suffered long and wasted years of precious time doing similar things and expecting dissimilar results. These were all the effects of convoluted concepts of a Christianity that attempts to define Christ. However...

Christianity cannot define Christ,
it is Christ that defines our Christianity.

Without Christ as our definitive, our Christianity amounts to nothing more than idols we shape in the image of a Christ as we imagine Him to be. This form of Christianity will never possess Christ's likeness. In all truth, these idealities are only the images we have of our best ideas of ourselves, none of which reflect the Christ of the Bible nor represent what Christ offers.

God the Father, Christ the Son, Lord Holy
Spirit will never accept being treated like
another object to be idolized.

We have made a mockery of the Scriptures. We have caused the Gospel great violence and have defaced the image and likeness of Christ to whom we are predestined to conform. These platitudes only contain contentious modalities marked by conditional faith and insufficient grace. The only cure to these maladies is a humble confession and a rejection of those very idols that we hold dear to our heart.

Now here is the scary truth. These idols are such great replicas of Christ that identifying them as counterfeit is virtually impossible for the individual to self-assess. These imposters are cunning and brilliantly integrated with emotional power we have associate with Holy Spirit in experience. Tearing down these idols requires taking losses.

Gideon was commanded by God to tear down the idols of Baal and Ashtoroth. He was also commanded to give up a fattened bull during a time where there was a famine and food was hard to come by. The emotional attachment to our idols will always come as a hurt or a hardship when we tear away from them. Yet, God asks Gideon to build an altar in dedication to Him with these very items. God takes those losses and makes greater appropriations. Allow me to clarify.

The idols Gideon tore down where made of wood, mortar, and stone. The wood, the mortar, and stone contained neither life nor substance. Yet, when given value, a level of importance is placed upon them. As a result, these inanimate objects are now viewed as greater than they are actually worth. The level of importance place upon them does not cause them to gain a greater value. The level of importance placed upon them serves only to devalue a level of worth from those who place that value upon them.

> **When we erect idols in our lives, we essentially give up our worth by pouring out our own worth into these empty objects and create a value in them.**

Simply put, for an object of no significant value to become valuable, one must place their own worth into it to give it life, cause it substance, and to regard it as important. Our importance becomes its value. An idol possesses no value until and unless we pour our importance or our worth into it.

The opposite of this is also true. When we retain our worth, an idol cannot possess value. Consider how when we let go of an issue, concern, hurt, or place no further importance into an item we have toiled over for such a long period of time, we experience a shift in our psyche, gain a refreshed sense of self-esteem, and find *worth* again. When worth is returned to its proper place, the idol is of zero value.

We are the only creatures of all creation that are not only created in God's image, but who are also called to bear God's likeness. By pouring out His own worth, God gave us life, caused us substance, and regarded us as important. In essence, He pours *worth* into us.

The work of salvation was never an entitlement extended to us. Heaven is not earned on effort. There is no good work that will outweigh our bad work that will result in gained entrance into heaven. Nor did Christ give up His own life because He decided that some of us are more deserving of heaven than others. Christ endured the cross because He saw each and every one of us as worth the cost of bearing the torment of the cross. Again, God pours worth into us.

We are saved by faith. We walk through Grace. And only those who will embrace salvation through Christ Jesus will receive eternal life. The journey to heaven is set at Christ's cross but our journey actually begins when we pick up our own cross.

As we come to a close, let me share with you a reflection I have adopted from a precious and powerful prayer warrior I had the privilege of getting to know, sister Nerys Rivera-Rosario. This reflection functions like my rear-view mirror, allowing me to only take a glimpse at what remains behind me, but serves to keep my eyes on what is before me. I hope this reflection will do the same for you.

"As I awaken I always wait expectantly for your voice calling to my spirit...
Here it is the dawn of a new day...
My Father who gifts me with the promise always of a fresh beginning...
As the dawn streaks the sky all that is bare holds the promise it will blossom...
All that is dormant within me holds the promise I, too, will bloom...
The beauty of the rising sun that fills my soul and yes the dawning of the new day...
And in my spirit I hear, "Here it is, My Promise...
"Receive beloveds!"
His gift, your new day!
And, He sits upon the throne and says,
"I am making everything new."

- Nerys Rivera-Rosario."

CPSIA information can be obtained
at www.ICGtesting.com
Printed in the USA
BVHW081011221121
622233BV00003B/136

9 781662 830211